THE C.S. LEWIS INST

PRESENTS

Heart
AND MIND
DISCIPLESHIP

A 10-week, small group program providing
fundamental truth for authentic spiritual growth

PUBLISHED BY:
C.S. Lewis Institute
8001 Braddock Road
Suite 301
Springfield, VA 22151
www.cslewisinstitute.org
information@cslewisinstitute.org

COMPILING AUTHOR & EDITOR:
Joel S. Woodruff, Ed.D.

DESIGN BY:
The Perspectives Group
www.theperspectivesgroup.com

ADDITIONAL DESIGN BY:
Karen J. Adams

ISBN: 978-1-939477-02-6

TABLE OF CONTENTS

INTRODUCTION

Welcome to the C.S. Lewis Institute's *Heart and Mind Discipleship* study series for small groups, produced with support from Alpha USA and Ravi Zacharias International Ministries (RZIM).

For more than thirty-five years, the C.S. Lewis Institute (CSLI) has been working to help Christian men and women to grow in their ability to defend, articulate, and live their Christian faith both in personal and public life. To accomplish this vision, CSLI has developed, evaluated, and refined discipleship programs that have been judged to be highly effective by Christian leaders from many denominational backgrounds. We have held seminars and conferences on discipleship. We have launched an intensive discipleship program in the greater Washington, D.C., area. This Fellows Program is now being offered in other cities, even internationally. The articles in our quarterly journal, *Knowing & Doing*, and our monthly devotional, "Reflections," also provide readers insights into the discipline of discipleship (to subscribe to these free publications, visit our website at: www.cslewisinstitute.org).

In recent years, church leaders have observed and reputable research has confirmed that the church in the West is, as some say, a mile wide and an inch deep. In other words, there is a dearth of spiritual growth and maturity in the church today; many believers remain infants in the faith and live no differently than their non-Christian neighbors. Because of this, the C.S. Lewis Institute rose to the challenge set before us: to develop a discipleship curriculum to be used by churches, small groups, campus ministries, and other Christian organizations to help ground believers in the foundational principles of Christian discipleship.

This *Heart and Mind Discipleship* workbook and DVD curriculum is our response to that challenge. It is ideal for new believers who may have gone through their church's basic Christianity course or participated in the popular and effective Alpha course. It is also helpful to anyone who has not been discipled in any significant way and to believers desiring to review and reestablish their understanding of their faith and grow into more mature disciples of Jesus Christ.

> *Any new resource needs to be "field-tested" and refined as needed. It is our plan to seek feedback from those who use this resource so we can continually improve the effectiveness of this resource over the coming years. As you participate in this* Heart and Mind Discipleship *study, please share with us your overall comments and any suggestions for improvement. Thank you.*

THE PROGRAM APPROACH

Heart and Mind Discipleship: In this era the amount of knowledge we can know doubles every couple of years. And yet humankind doesn't seem to be any wiser; the same problems and sins that abounded thousands of years ago are still with us today. Knowledge is important, but if it's not applied in a wise manner it won't make us better people. In the same way, the disciple of Jesus Christ has to be careful about one of two extremes: living a zealous life for God without taking the time to learn biblical truth or amassing biblical knowledge without applying God's wisdom to one's daily life. This is why the C.S. Lewis Institute emphasizes discipleship of heart *and* mind. As believers grow in their knowledge of God's Word and also mature in their application of it in their personal and public life, they will be more effective and more fulfilled disciples. Many have grown up in the church and yet have never been challenged or taught how to integrate biblical truth into their daily lives. This study seeks to engage the believer at two levels, the heart and mind; more than just another academic exercise, it is designed to help people serve the Lord and their neighbor as they are empowered by the Holy Spirit.

The Purpose: The goal of the *Heart and Mind Discipleship* program is to provide the church and home groups with a resource that will enable new converts and those who desire to grow in their faith to take that "next step" toward Christian maturity and discipleship.

The Program Components: The following components of the *Heart and Mind Discipleship* program are designed to provide a ten-week high-quality, high-impact curriculum that focuses on that "next step" in Christian discipleship, spiritual formation, and mission.

- **Teaching on DVD:** These thirty-minute presentations are taught by recognized authorities in the area of Christian discipleship. These powerful communicators have pastoral wisdom and sensitivity and are by God's grace trying to live what they teach. Each DVD can be watched together by the small group and should provide engaging material for group discussion following the presentation.

- **Bible Study Questions:** Prior to the showing of the DVD, group members are encouraged to work individually to complete the Bible study based on key biblical passages apropos to the theme of the week. The Bible study is a key component to the program, which foundationally urges believers to spend time in their primary source of learning—the Bible.

- **Scripture Memory Verse:** There is nothing like storing God's written Word in your heart. By memorizing the theme verse for the week, group participants will be absorbing the teaching in both their hearts and minds. Reciting the verse

INTRODUCTION

together as a group or in pairs during the group meeting is a helpful way to do this. Participants are also encouraged to meditate upon these verses throughout the week.

- **Thoughtful Articles on the Weekly Theme:** These short articles that complement the DVD lectures are written by experienced Christian leaders and writers. The intent of the articles is to synthesize the theme of the week and lay out a broader outline of the material. We recommend that individuals read the article before the group study.

- **Discussion Questions for Small Group:** Suggested questions have been provided to facilitate the small group discussion following the group viewing of the DVD. The questions take into account the DVD material, the thematic article, the memory verse, and individual Bible study.

- **Leader's Agenda for Weekly Small Group:** A suggested format for each week's small group meeting is provided in the leader's guide. This will provide the facilitator of the study with practical ideas and questions to help the group tease out the important truths and ideas of each week's study.

Program Delivery Methods: The combination of auditory, kinesthetic, and visual delivery methods enables people to learn the material in multiple ways and serves to reinforce the teachings. What's more, the insights gained from individual study can be refined and shared in small group study as the Holy Spirit guides the discussion. The hope is that the students will learn and apply these truths of Christian discipleship to their hearts and minds and be better able to live out their faith in both personal and public life. In other words, the goal is to come out of this program speaking and acting more like Jesus in daily life.

Program Topics by Week: The program can be completed in ten weeks by covering one topic per week and combining topics 6A & 6B in week 6. Or it can be completed in eleven weeks by studying one topic per week.

1. God's Character & Personality
2. God's Story of Redemption
3. Understanding Salvation
4. God's Plan for Our Growth
5. The Cost of Discipleship
6A. Humility & Servanthood and 6B. Loving God & Neighbor
7. Authority of the Bible
8. The Practice of Prayer
9. The Mission of the Church
10. Sharing the Good News

In Conclusion: The *Heart and Mind Discipleship* study series is designed to help churches and individuals sharpen their focus on spiritual maturity and discipleship—and to be an easy-to-replicate discipleship program that can reach a wide variety of Christian churches, ministries, and groups. Our prayer at CSLI is that the study's multisensory educational methods, engaging teachers, and thoughtful materials will be an effective tool in developing mature disciples of Christ.

SAMPLE SMALL GROUP STUDY AGENDA (TOTAL: 90 MINUTES)	
10 Minutes	Social Time
5 Minutes	Introduction of Topic and Prayer
30 Minutes	Play DVD Teaching
35 Minutes	Discussion Questions
10 Minutes	Closing: Recite Memory Verse & Prayer Time

HOME GROUP DINNER AND STUDY MODEL (TOTAL: 120 MINUTES)	
40 Minutes	Simple Dinner and Social Time (Pizza, Salad, Drinks, and Desserts—or a potluck)
5 Minutes	Introduction of Topic and Prayer
30 Minutes	Play DVD Teaching
35 Minutes	Discussion Questions
10 Minutes	Closing: Recite Memory Verse & Prayer Time

SUNDAY SCHOOL CLASS/ WORKPLACE MODEL	
5 Minutes	Introduction of Topic and Prayer
30 Minutes	Play DVD Teaching
25–55 Minutes	Discussion Questions, Memory Verse & Prayer Time

Chapter 1

Speaker Bio:
Stuart McAlpine

Teaching Fellow, C.S. Lewis Institute – Stuart is the founding pastor of Christ Our Shepherd Church located on Capitol Hill in Washington, D.C. He speaks at churches and conferences around the world and also lectures for the C.S. Lewis Institute Fellows Program. He has a great knowledge of, and love for, the works of C.S. Lewis. He holds a bachelor's degree in English literature and a master's degree in theology from Cambridge University in Great Britain.

Author Bio:
Stephen Eyre, M. Div

Director, C.S. Lewis Institute - Cincinnati – Stephen Eyre has served both in college campus ministry and pastoral ministry for more than twenty years. He has written numerous books, Bible study guides, and devotional books that have been published nationally and internationally through Inter-Varsity Press, Zondervan, and Victor Press. Stephen has written several study guides for C.S. Lewis Institute publications including *Mere Christianity, Screwtape Letters,* and *Letters to Malcolm; Chiefly on Prayer,* as well as the Bible Study Questions for this publication. He earned a B.A. in history from Clearwater Christian College and a M.Div. from Covenant Theological Seminary.

GOD'S CHARACTER AND PERSONALITY

Who is God? What is God like? Our understanding of God shapes not only our faith, but our entire approach to life, our values and priorities. Unfortunately, many have a distorted view of God and this has led to many of the problems that we have in society, the church, and our personal lives. Rather than getting to know the loving and holy God revealed in the Scriptures, false notions of God have infiltrated our thinking from other religions, philosophy, media, and family traditions. These incorrect views of God hinder us from fully surrendering ourselves to him and being as effective in sharing his love with others. The intent of this study is to help us recover a biblical understanding of the character and personality of God so that we can love, trust and serve him in a more faithful, fruitful, and fulfilling way.

CHAPTER 1 – GOD'S CHARACTER AND PERSONALITY

Thomas Aquinas called theology the "queen of sciences." But the study of theology—the study of God—was gradually sidelined and now finds no place in the contemporary curriculum. Alexander Pope captured the spirit of our modern age:

> Know then thyself, presume not God to scan;
> The proper study of Mankind is Man.

I have come to disagree with Mr. Pope. Focusing first on "Man" can get you into trouble. When I was in college, it was fashionable to have an identity crisis. Leaving family, rejecting friends, staying in school or dropping out—any behavior was fair game as long as it contributed to the task of "finding" yourself. Not what it was cracked up to be, looking for yourself led to a descent down the rabbit hole, into a terrifyingly confused "Wonderland" filled with smiling Cheshire cats, Mad Hatters, and insane queens shouting "off with your head."

Knowing God is what makes sense of life. Missing God leads to disaster. In his classic book *Knowing God*, J.I. Packer writes:

> The world becomes a strange, mad, painful place, and life in it a disappointing and unpleasant business for those who do not know about God. Disregard the study of God and you sentence yourself to stumble and blunder through life blindfolded as it were with no sense of direction and no understanding of what surrounds you. This way you can waste your life and lose your soul.[1]

In contrast to Mr. Pope, the famous first question of the Westminster Confession asks, "What is the chief end of man?" The wonderful answer is "To glorify God and enjoy him forever."

Prior to my conversion, I had the impression that the study of theology was arid, intellectual, dry, and boring. I couldn't have been more wrong. The pursuit of the knowledge of God has introduced me to great people, great authors, great ministries, and great thoughts.

Ever since then I have been on a journey to learn as much as I can about this God who called me. I am a pastor, but I didn't go to seminary in order to enter the ministry. (During those first days of my Christian walk, I would lie in bed awake, fearful that God might require me to be a minister or a missionary.) I went for theological study because I wanted to learn more about God.

Frankly, it is good to know God. It's how we learn to make sense of the world and especially of our selves. Protestant Reformer John Calvin wrote, "Our wisdom ... consists almost entirely of two parts: the knowledge of God and of ourselves."[2] He continues, "By the knowledge of God, I understand that by which we not only conceive that there is some God, but also apprehend what it is for our interest."[3]

So how do we get to know this God so that we can enjoy him? As Christians we believe that God has not left us to wander in the dark. Daily, moment by moment, all that he has created points to and speaks of him. As David wrote, "The heavens declare the glory of God ... even if there are no words, they continually speak of him" (Ps. 19:1, 3). Part of the satisfaction of studying about God is learning to experience the fullness of his presence. The knowledge of God is all around us if only we could see it. Gerard Manley Hopkins enthused, "The world is charged with the grandeur of God."

If we are to learn to hear silent declarations of creation, we need help. While the heavens declare the glory of God, they don't declare his name, that is, his personality and character. The existence of multiple religions makes it clear that mankind can and has drawn many different conclusions about who God is and what he is like.

GOD IN THE BIBLE

If you want to know what a new acquaintance is like, it is wise to pay attention to what he or she tells you and to observe that person's actions. This is what we have in the Bible: God's self-revelation in which he speaks about himself and provides a record over generations and ages about how he acts.

The first five books of the Bible are attributed to Moses. Often called the Pentateuch (Greek for "Five Scrolls") or the Torah (Hebrew for "Law"), they are the foundation for the entire Bible. Hebrew by birth, Egyptian by culture, royal by training, and desert shepherd by necessity, Moses was providentially shaped to be an agent of revelation, a prophet.

Imagine Moses' first impression of God as he meets God in the flames of a burning bush. Light, heat, energy, power! God is more than a concept or an idea; he is a person, a shining presence who speaks as we meet him in the fabric of creation.

In the account of Exodus 3, the very first action required of Moses is that he must take his sandals off because he is standing on "holy ground" (v. 5). The holiness of God is a central thread woven throughout the Bible, exemplified again in Moses' encounter with God on Mount Sinai, the vision of the prophet Isaiah some seven hundred years later (Isa. 6:3), and the apostle John's vision of heaven (Rev. 4:8).

Holiness is a mysterious concept that is hard to nail down. Words associated with it include: *unmixed, unpolluted, uncorrupted, separate, unique, just, righteous, sacred, precious,* and *honored.* Holiness was not just for the Old Testament. Jesus makes the holiness of God central, as the prayer he teaches us begins, "Our Father in heaven, holy is your name" (Matt. 6:9).

Meeting with God as the holy God, for Moses and for all ever since, is a life-changing experience. R.C. Sproul describes his first encounter with God. As college student, he was awakened and summoned from his bed in the middle of the night. At first he was overwhelmed with fear by a "foreboding presence." As the fright subsided, he sensed a different "wave."

> It flooded my soul with unspeakable peace, a peace that brought instant rest and repose to my troubled spirit. At once I wanted to linger there. To say nothing. To do nothing. Simply to bask in the presence of God.

> That moment was life transforming. Something deep in my spirit was being settled once for all. From this moment there could be no turning back; there could be no erasure of the indelible imprint of its power. I was alone with God. A holy God. An awesome God. A God who could fill me with terror in one second and fill with peace the next.[4]

It might be helpful to reflect on how God first got your attention. God is a God who steps into our world, interrupts us, and calls us to himself and his purposes. Clearly this is what we see in the ministry of Jesus as Jesus walks into the fishing sites of Peter, James, John, and Andrew by the sea of Galilee and says, "Follow me and I will make you fish for people" (Mark 1:16, NRSV).

Immediately after declaring his holiness at the burning bush, God identifies himself as the God of Abraham, Isaac, and Jacob (Exod. 3:6). Look closely at this self-description of God. Growing up as a Hebrew in an Egyptian household, among people who worshiped many different gods, Moses' view of God up to this point would have been influenced by a variety of sources. Unlike today, when the common question for many is "do I believe in God?" the question for Moses would have been "which god do I worship?"

You may not think that you face the same sort of question that Moses did. After all, we don't live in a polytheistic society. But the "many gods" now masquerade as "belief systems" and "theological inclinations." Liberal, conservative, secular, modern, Muslim, Mormon, Buddhist, atheist, agnostic—it's everywhere! Each of us, consciously or unconsciously, makes choices about which god to worship.

God chose to make his character known to Moses by associating himself with certain people Moses knew about: Abraham, Isaac, and Jacob. Those stories, passed down through the generations of the Hebrews, told about a certain God who provided, protected, and blessed—the accounts we read in the book of Genesis. As God has chosen to make himself known by association, there are people in your life, sent by God, who provide important information about what God is like. Pay attention to them.

To Moses at the burning bush, God also reveals what he is like when he says, "I have indeed seen the misery of my people ... So I have come down to rescue them" (vv. 7–8). Like holiness, salvation is a theme that runs through the Bible. The Israelites' exodus from Egypt shows us something significant about the character of God: he is a saving God. This stands in stark contrast to the gods of the Egyptians, Greeks, Romans, or Babylonians who were not especially interested in saving anybody. Saving Israel from slavery in Egypt by Moses, saving us from spiritual slavery to sin and Satan, God is not willing for his creation to become co-opted and corrupted and to be in a place of enduring pain and misery. Mary celebrates the saving character of God when the angel announces the coming birth of her son. "My spirit rejoices in God my Savior" (Luke 1:47).

I love the way the psalms celebrate the character of God.

> *The LORD is gracious and compassionate, slow to anger and rich in love. The LORD is good to all; he has compassion on all he has made ... The LORD is faithful to all his promises and loving toward all he has made. The LORD upholds all those who fall and lifts up all who are bowed down. (145:8–9, 13–14)*

God is holy. God is the God of his ancestors. God is a saving God—these are important pieces of information for Moses. But there is more: Moses wants to know God's name (v. 13). It's the ultimate question, because we can't claim to know anybody if we don't know that person's name. Think about brand names; they convey the importance of a name. Car, shoe, guitar are generic names. We know a great deal more when we know the brand name: BMW, Nike, Martin.

The name God provides is not generic; it is his brand. He is not just any god, he is "I AM WHO I AM" (v. 14). Commentators struggle to mine its meaning. "I Am the One Who Is" or "I Am the One Whom You Shall Know" are two of the proposed options. "I Am" is how God wants to be addressed.

C.S. Lewis's portrayal of Aslan in the Chronicles of Narnia portrays the wonder and thrill of hearing God name himself.

> "Who are you?" asked Shasta.

> "Myself," said the Voice, very deep and low so that the earth shook: and again, "Myself," loud and clear and gay: and then the third time "Myself," whispered so softly you could hardly hear it, and yet it seemed to come from all round you as if the leaves rustled with it ...

> ... After one glance at the Lion's face he slipped out of the saddle and fell at its feet. He couldn't say anything but then he didn't want to say anything.[5]

God has revealed himself most completely through Jesus Christ. The first Christians came to the conclusion that Jesus is "the image of the invisible God" (Col. 1:15). That is, Jesus is the "visible God" and reliably embodies the character of God (Heb. 1:3). If you want to know God, pay close attention to Jesus, who he is, what he taught, what he did. Reflecting on God from the Old Testament to the New, the church through the ages discovered a complex being, a triune God, a Trinity of persons comprising one God: Father, Son, and Holy Spirit.

What we take away from our theological reflection is that I have a Creator who provides for me, protects me, has purposes for me, and has a place for me in his world. In God I have a Savior who rescues me from the problems of the corrupted world. In God I have a Holy Spirit who indwells me: he provides insight, inspiration, encouragement, inspiration, and empowerment.

The God revealed in the Bible from the first lines of Genesis 1 is the Maker, the Craftsman, the Workman, the Governor, the Speaker ... How different from the unmoved mover of Greek philosophy or the "higher power" that stands and watches us from a distance. *Your God Is Too Small* is the title of a great little book written in the middle of the twentieth century. No matter who we are and at what stage of our spiritual journey, we can all say that the way we think about God isn't big enough.

THE PURSUIT OF GOD

The desire to know and proclaim the knowledge of God is not only what the Bible is about. It is the subject of innumerable books—filling libraries. The mystery of God draws us. Consider Augustine's take:

> You awake us to delight in your praise; for you made us for yourself, and our heart is restless, until it rests in you.[6]

> What, therefore, is my God? ... most secret and most truly present ... unchangeable, yet changing all things; never new, never old; ... always working, ever at rest; gathering, yet needing nothing ... You love, but without passion; jealous, yet free from care; repents without remorse; angry, yet remains serene.[7]

The Westminster Catechism, written in the seventeenth century to instruct children in the knowledge of God, succinctly and memorably asks the question and provides the answer.

> Question: What is God?
> Answer: God is a Spirit, infinite, eternal, and unchangeable, in his being, wisdom, power, holiness, justice, goodness, and truth.

Writing in the twentieth century, A.W. Tozer notes:

> God is a Person, and in the deep of His mighty nature He thinks, wills, enjoys, feels, loves, desires and suffers as any other person may ... The continuous and unembarrassed interchange of love and thought between God and the soul of the redeemed man is the throbbing heart of New Testament religion.[8]

St. Anselm in the twelfth century said that study of God was "faith, seeking understanding." The whole history of the church shows that knowing God is a journey of delight and desire. St. Bernard in the thirteenth century said it this way:

> We taste thee, O thou Living Bread,
> And long to feast upon thee still:
> We drink of thee, the Fountainhead
> And thirst our souls from thee to fill.

The knowledge of the triune God is not something we merely possess, but something that possesses us. Tozer challenges us to:

> Come near to the holy men and women of the past and you will soon feel the heat of their desire after God. They mourned for Him, they prayed and wrestled and sought for Him day and night, in season and out, and when they had found Him the finding was all the sweeter for the long seeking.

The pursuit of the knowledge of God is not a duty or a drudge, but a journey filled with bright and shining light that leads to enjoyment and pleasure, now and for all eternity.

NOTES

[1] J.I. Packer, *Knowing God* (Downers Grove, IL: InterVarsity Press, 1973), 15.

[2] John Calvin, *The Institutes of the Christian Religion* I.1.1.

[3] Ibid., I.2.1.

[4] R.C. Sproul, *The Holiness of God* (Wheaton: Tyndale House, 1998), 5.

[5] C.S. Lewis, *The Horse and His Boy* (New York: Macmillan/Collier, 1970), 160.

[6] Augustine, *The Confessions of Augustine* I.1.

[7] Ibid., I.4.

[8] A.W. Tozer, *The Pursuit of God*, (SoHo Books 2011), 6.

[9] Ibid., 7.

Scripture Memory Verse

The Lord is compassionate and gracious, slow to anger, abounding in love. (Psalm 103:8, NIV)

Bible Study Questions

Exodus 34:1–14

"What comes into your mind when you think about God is the most important thing about you." — A.W. Tozer

A lot came into Moses' mind when he thought about God. From the first encounter at the burning bush, Moses—the agent of God's plagues of judgment, the receiver of the Torah, the national leader through the desert to the Promised Land—walked with God as few ever have. Read Exodus 34:1–14.

1. Holy is one of the essential words to describe the God of the Bible. Although the word is not used in this text, the holiness of God is woven through every verse. What do you glean about the holiness of God as you read this passage?

_____

_____

_____

_____

2. What insights about God's holy character come to mind from the stipulations that (a) access to Mount Sinai be restricted (vv. 2–3) and (b) the people are not to mix with the other nations (vv. 11–14)?

_____

_____

_____

_____

3. What can you do to cultivate and encourage an awareness of the holiness of God?

_____

_____

_____

_____

4. God reveals key aspects of his character in verses 4-7. How does his grace, compassion, patience, love and faithfulness show up in the life of Christ on earth? What do the chiseled stone tablets contribute to our knowledge of God?

_____

_____

_____

_____

5. While clouds, the heavens, and all of nature declare the glory of God, they are limited as means of spiritual insight because they don't declare his "name." However, God does declare his name as he stands with Moses (vv. 5–6). What does God declaring his name reveal about his character?

_____

_____

_____

_____

6. Considering how God chose to describe himself (vv. 5–9), what do you find comforting? What do you find challenging?

_____

_____

_____

_____

7. How do you think Moses understood and acted on his understanding of God's character based on his prayer (vv.8-9)? How do you act upon God's description of himself?

_____

_____

_____

_____

8. What is comforting and challenging about being in a relationship with a God who makes and keeps a covenant (v. 10)?

_____

_____

_____

_____

9. In contrast to the gods of the Egyptians, Canaanites, Babylonians, Romans, and Greeks who didn't seem to mind sharing the limelight, God describes himself as jealous (vv. 11–14)! What would it say about God's character if he didn't care whether the people to whom he committed himself were committed to him?

_____

_____

_____

_____

10. Considering this passage as a whole, it is fair to say that a relationship with a holy, covenant-making God is a solemn and awesome responsibility. Why is it also a wonder-full, awe-some, and thrilling privilege?

_____

_____

_____

_____

GROUP DISCUSSION QUESTIONS

1. What are some of the false notions of God that you have heard expressed in the media, within your family, and in the church? How do these false concepts of God negatively affect the way people live and act?

    _____

    _____

2. What are some of the essential character traits of God as revealed in the Bible? Define these traits.

    _____

    _____

3. If you had to give an elevator talk (1 minute) about who God is and what God is like, how would you do it?

    _____

    _____

4. Where has your view of God perhaps been out of line with how he has revealed himself in Scripture? What changes will you need to make to embrace the biblical view?

    _____

    _____

5. How can a misunderstanding about God affect the way that you are able to love God and other people? Give some examples.

    _____

    _____

6. How does understanding the true character of God help us deal with the problems in our lives, the church and society? Conflict? Injustice? Personal hardship?

    _____

    _____

7. Give examples of how a correct view of God's character and personality could change the church, your family, and society.

    _____

    _____

8. What habits might help us develop a more solid understanding of the truth about God's character and personality? How can we put those habits into practice this week?

    _____

    _____

CHAPTER 2

SPEAKER BIO: WILLIAM "BILL" KYNES, PH.D.

SENIOR FELLOW, C.S. LEWIS INSTI-TUTE – Bill Kynes is the senior pastor of Cornerstone, an Evangelical Free Church, in Annandale, Virginia, where he has served since 1986. He was an undergraduate at the University of Florida with a major in philosophy. There he also played quarterback on the football team and was later inducted into the university's Athletic Hall of Fame. He attended Oxford University as a Rhodes Scholar, receiving an M.A. in theology. He received an M.Div. from Trinity Evangelical Divinity School, in Deerfield, Illinois, before returning to England for a Ph.D. in New Testament from Cambridge University.

AUTHOR BIO: STEPHEN EYRE, M.DIV.

DIRECTOR, C.S. LEWIS INSTITUTE - CINCINNATI – Stephen Eyre has served both in college campus ministry and pastoral ministry for more than twenty years. He has written numerous books, Bible study guides, and devotional books that have been published nationally and internationally through Inter-Varsity Press, Zondervan, and Victor Press. Stephen has written several study guides for C.S. Lewis Institute publications including *Mere Christianity, Screwtape Letters,* and *Letters to Malcolm; Chiefly on Prayer*, as well as the Bible Study Questions for this publication. He earned a B.A. in history from Clearwater Christian College and a M.Div. from Covenant Theological Seminary.

GOD'S STORY OF REDEMPTION

Everyone likes a good story. This may be due to the fact that we as human beings are created in the image of God – the Great Storyteller – who has revealed himself to us through the Bible, through his Son, Jesus Christ, and through the beauty of his creation. God's story of creation, the fall of humankind, redemption, and consummation is the most compelling story of all time. Yet, there are many competing stories surrounding us today in the world that falsely claim to offer a better tale. It's only in reading and listening to God's story of redemption that we will finally be able to get the real scoop on such questions as "where do I come from?" "where am I going?" and "what is the meaning of life?" We hope that as you contemplate the beautiful story of God's redemption of humankind, you will come to see it as the greatest story ever told.

The Bible is a large and complex book—sixty-six books written over a thousand years. You can get lost trying to make sense of it. However, it is possible to divide the Bible simply into thirds and see its essential theme:

- Genesis 1–2 comprises the first third of the Bible in which we read about God's good world.

- Revelation 21–22 comprises the last third of the Bible in which God's good world is restored.

- The middle third, and the bulk of the material, is about what God is doing to bring the world back to his original intention.

CREATION	FALL AND REDEMPTION	CONSUMMATION
Genesis 1–2	Most of the Bible	Revelation 21–22

Once we understand the way the world was supposed to be, the way it is now, and the way it will one day be again, we have tools to make sense of our life experiences and our longings. Without such a broad biblical perspective, our pains may seem depressively terminal and our longings and joys frustratingly empty.

CREATION

I hate to walk into a movie after it has started. If I stay, I stick around until the next showing to see the beginning. Sure enough, even though I was able to make sense of most of the action, I find pieces of the plot that I didn't get. Since the book of Genesis is about the beginning of the world, until you are familiar with it, you too will be missing pieces of life. What does it tell us about our origins?

1. God exists before and beyond the world he creates.

In the beginning God created the heavens and the earth. (1:1)[1]

We might be tempted to think that Genesis 1–2 is just about creation. But it is primarily about God. Skim Genesis 1 and note the references to God: "And God said" (v. 3); "God saw" (v. 4); "God called" (v. 5); "And God said" (v. 6); "So God made" (v. 7); "God called" (v. 8), and so on through the rest of the chapter. Deism, which arose in the seventeenth century, and naturalism and evolution, in the eighteenth and nineteenth centuries, offer ways of conceiving of the world in which God is distantly removed or absent all together.

The depiction of God in Genesis is also in contrast to pantheism of the East, in which everything is God, and pan-in-theism, in which God is in everything. From Genesis we can see that God is never synonymous with his world. He is before it, will be after it, and, while involved in it, stands above and outside it.

The Genesis account teaches us that we are never to think about the world without thinking about it as God's world. John Calvin said that the world is "the theater of God's glory" and observed that it is not possible to conceive of the world as God's creation without experiencing a desire to honor him. Beyond that, we should believe that our greatest good is in knowing him.

Moreover although our mind cannot apprehend God without rendering some honor to him, it will not suffice simply to hold that he is the One whom all ought to honor and adore, unless we are also persuaded that he is the fountain of every good and that we must seek nothing elsewhere than in him.[2]

> 2. God orders his world.

Now the earth was formless and empty, darkness was over the surface of the deep. (1:2)

This sentence provides the structure to all that follows. In the initial stage of creation, the earth was "formless" and "empty." In the rest of Genesis 1 God forms and fills his world. A simple chart shows the structure of the creation days.

GENESIS 1

FORMED	FILLED
1. Light, vv. 3–5	4. Luminaries, vv. 14–19
2. Sky and water, vv. 6–8	5. Birds and fish, vv. 20–23
3. Land, vv. 9–13	6. Land animals, vv. 24–28

God unfolds and develops his creation in an orderly way through the course of his work week. This description of creation as a literary structure provides true information about the Creator and the process by which he forms and fills his world.

3. God makes the world good.

The word *good* is used seven times in Genesis 1, in verses 3, 9, 12, 18, 21, 25, 31. As created, the world is not fractured or corrupted. God likes and takes pleasure in it. In God's world, as originally created, it was good to be alive.

Neither Socrates nor the Buddha, nor the systems of thought attributed to them, considered the world good. Both taught that final pleasure involved escaping this world, into a spiritual, nonphysical state.

4. God makes humanity in his image.

So God created man in his own image ... male and female he created them. (v. 27)

Made in God's image on the sixth day, humans share, in common, the nature of the other land animals.

God. | Humans. Animals.

Made in the image of God, humans are unique; different from the rest of creation.

God. Humans. | Animals.

The Fall

The world described in Genesis 1–2 does not continue. Our daily experience confirms this. It is worth noting that the first explicitly Christian book that C.S. Lewis wrote was titled *The Problem of Pain*. We live in a world that is a swirl of both pleasure and pain. Where did this pain come from?

In Genesis 3 we read that the world was corrupted by the invasion of evil, through the choice of God's king and queen. Goodness is now polluted by that which is bad, and the image of God, gloriously radiating in his world, is now fractured. Let's look more closely at the text of Genesis 3.

1. God sets limits.

God set limits, and Eve knew it. She exaggerated the limits but nevertheless stated the prohibition: "God did say, 'You must not eat fruit from the tree that is the middle of the garden, and you must not touch it, or you will die'" (v. 3).

Just as a game makes no sense without rules and referees, God makes the rules and is the referee. He had said, in effect, "Enjoy the garden but don't eat the fruit from one tree; if you do, you will die."

2. A hostile being is present in the world and raises suspicion about God's character.

Now the serpent was more crafty than any of the wild animals that the LORD God had made. (v. 1)

Satan is a liar in a twofold sense; first, he calls into question the character of God.

Did God really say, "You must not eat from any tree in the garden"? (v. 1)

For God knows that when you eat of it your eyes will be opened, and you will be like God, knowing good and evil. (v. 4)

The implication of the serpent is that God has good things available that he is withholding. God is, Satan implies, mean and stingy.

Second, Satan is a liar in the sense that he blatantly, directly contradicts God, "You will not surely die" (v. 4).

John Milton, in *Paradise Lost* (Book 9), explores the infernal dynamics that defiled Satan in eternity.

Forth reaching to the Fruit, she pluk'd, she eat:
Earth felt the wound, and Nature from her seat
Sighing through all her Works gave signs of woe,
That all was lost. Back to the Thicket slunk
The guilty Serpent.

What we read in Genesis 3 about the insulations of Satan continues to the present; quietly, subtly, constantly, Satan continues to lie about the character of God and the truth of God's Word.

3. Adam and Eve break faith with God and overstep their limits.

When the woman saw that the fruit of the tree was good for food and pleasing to the eye, and also desirable for gaining wisdom, she took some and ate it. She also gave some to her husband, who was with her, and he ate it. (vv. 6–7)

Augustine and many since him attribute the invasion of evil into the world to the pride of our first royal parents—reaching for more than they were given. In *Mere Christianity* C.S. Lewis agrees that pride was the chief sin. Martin Luther, who rediscovered the role of faith in salvation, was convinced that lack of faith was the chief sin. Adam and Eve didn't believe God when warned of death. They chose to believe Satan. Instead of enjoying the goodness in which they were immersed, they believed that God was holding out on them.

Since that day, God has been on trial. The problem of pain and evil is a reason many people give for denying or renouncing faith in God. But if you renounce God, you need to deal with the problem of goodness. How do we explain all that is good in the world and all the good that we desire to do if we were not created by a good God?

4. The intimate relationship between humans and God is fractured.

Then the man and his wife heard the sound of the LORD God as he was walking in the garden in the cool of the day, and they hid from the LORD God among the trees of the garden. But the LORD God called to the man, 'Where are you?' (vv. 8–9)

Adam and Eve enjoyed an evening walk with God. The picture is one of close friendship. Having broken faith, our first parents felt shame and hid among the bushes. As a race we have been hiding in the bushes ever since, loudly protesting that we can't find God.

What a chimera then is man! What a novelty!
What a monster, what a chaos, what a contradiction, what a prodigy!
Judge of all things, imbecile worm of the earth;
Depository of truth, a sink of uncertainty and error;
The pride and refuse of the universe ...

Know then, proud man, what a paradox you are to yourself.
Humble yourself, weak reason; be silent, foolish nature;
Learn that man infinitely transcends man
and learn from your Master your true condition,
of which you are ignorant.
Hear God.[4]

5. God curses his previously blessed world.

So the LORD God said to the serpent, "Because you have done this, Cursed are you" ... To the woman he said, "I will greatly increase your pains in childbearing" ... To Adam he said ... "Cursed is the ground because of you". (vv. 14–19)

God doesn't shout and show up with thunder and lightning; he patiently questions and pronounces judgment. Neither the wrath of God nor the curse is a popular subject. Yet God is angry about his polluted and corrupted world.

> *The wrath of God is being revealed from heaven against all the godlessness and wickedness of men who suppress the truth by their wickedness, since what may be known about God is plain to them, because God has made it plain to them. For since the creation of the world God's invisible qualities—his eternal power and divine nature—have been clearly seen, being understood from what has been made, so that men are without excuse. (Rom. 1:18–20)*

Imagine the pain God must have experienced cursing his good world! Who wants to admit we live in a cursed world? Yet it is the consistent theme of Scripture. How else can we explain that the good and sovereign God allows the pain and grief we now experience?

REDEMPTION

The God who patiently called Adam and Eve out of the bushes began his great work of salvation. God selects the family of Noah (Genesis 6–9). When the descendants of Noah seek to construct a civilization while ignoring God, he frustrates their efforts and confuses human language (Genesis 11). Then God selects Abraham (Genesis 12). Through the family of Abraham, God creates a line, the Hebrew nation, that over two thousand years will lead to the birth of a new Adam, Jesus Christ.

Step by step God saves us in Christ.

1. Through the act of becoming human, God himself assumes the image of God.
   The Son is the "image of the invisible God." (Col. 1:15)

2. *Where Adam failed the temptation, Jesus succeeded. (Luke 4:1–13)*
   Jesus answered, "It says: 'Do not put the Lord your God to the test.'" (Luke 4:12)

3. Then Jesus took the consequences of Adam's curse and died.
   When we were still powerless, Christ died for the ungodly. (Rom. 5:6)

4. When God raises Jesus from the dead, it's the beginning of the new creation; no more curse; no more death.
   For since death came through a man, the resurrection of the dead comes also through a man. (1 Cor. 15:21)

Therefore, if anyone is in Christ, he is a new creation; the old has gone, the new has come! (2 Cor. 5:17)

Jesus' proclamation of the kingdom of heaven (Matt. 4:17) is an announcement that through faith in him it is possible to enter the renewed creation.

The Spirit of the Lord is on me, because he has anointed me to proclaim good news to the poor. He has sent me to proclaim freedom for the prisoners and recovery of sight for the blind, to release the oppressed, to proclaim the year of the Lord's favor. (Luke 4:18–19)

The miracles that Jesus did—the healing of the sick, the opening of blinded eyes, the forgiving of sins, and the casting out of demons—all demonstrate the presence of the new creation.

5. Redemption is both complete and yet still in process.

Why then, do we still struggle with pain, sickness, and disappointment? Some of us are healed but not all of us. And healed or not, Christians still die. We experience growth in holiness, but we still struggle with the three classic enemies: the world, the flesh, and the devil.

In The Presence of the Kingdom, G.E. Ladd notes that we live in the intersection of two ages. The new age has come, but the old one has not yet been abolished. The new creation has been initiated but not yet completed. This means we live in the "yet/not yet," and the "here and coming." The kingdom of God, the new creation, has been initiated by Jesus, and we taste its fruits, but we are awaiting its consummation.

The Fallen and Fractured World   The Yet/Not Yet   The Restored and Re-created World

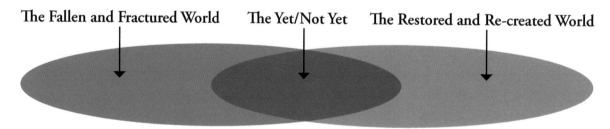

CONSUMMATION

The book of Revelation records the final battles in which the war for God's good creation is finally completed (chaps. 1–20). After the final victory over Satan, the old age is completely abolished. Revelation 21 describes a new order.

Then I saw a new heaven and a new earth, for the first heaven and the first earth had passed away, and there was no longer any sea. I saw the Holy City, the new Jerusalem,

coming down out of heaven from God, prepared as a bride beautifully dressed for her husband. And I heard a loud voice from the throne saying, "Now the dwelling of God is with men, and he will live with them. They will be his people, and God himself will be with them and be their God. He will wipe every tear from their eyes. There will be no more death or mourning or crying or pain, for the old order of things has passed away."

He who was seated on the throne said, "I am making everything new!" Then he said, "Write this down, for these words are trustworthy and true." (vv. 1–5)

Rev.

In that new world God will again be present among us; pain and death will be eradicated. Again, the tree of life will bear its fruit (22:2), and the curse will be no more (22:3). The renewed world will be completely safe, completely good and enjoyable.

The thrill of this new world beckons us: we can't wait to be refreshed, renewed, re-created, and restored. It is what every boy or girl really wants when gazing longingly at some desired toy or doll. It is what every adult wants when thinking of a new car, a new house, or a new job. G.K. Chesterton, in his pithy style, wrote, "Every knock on a brothel door is a knock on the door of heaven."

We are all waiting for that consummation. In the words of C.S. Lewis:

At present we are on the outside of the world, the wrong side of the door. We discern the freshness and purity of morning, but they do not make us fresh and pure. We cannot mingle with the splendours we see. But all the leaves of the New Testament are rustling with the rumour that it will not always be so. Someday, God willing, we shall get in.[5]

NOTES

[1]Unless otherwise noted, Scripture quotations are from the *New International Version*, 1984.

[2]John Calvin, *The Institutes of the Christian Religion* I.i.II.

[3]If the work of *Paradise Lost* is daunting, consider, C.S. Lewis, Preface to *Paradise Lost* (London: Oxford University Press, 1961), which makes accessible Milton's great thoughts on the Creation and Fall.

[4]Blaise Pascal, *Pensées* (London: Penguin Books, 1996) sec 434.

[5]C.S. Lewis, *The Weight of Glory*, quoted in C.S. Lewis, *A Year with C.S. Lewis* (San Francisco: HarperSanFrancisco, 2003), 397.

SCRIPTURE MEMORY VERSE

For God so loved the world that he gave his one and only Son, that whoever believes in him shall not perish but have eternal life. For God did not send his Son into the world to condemn the world, but to save the world through him.
(John 3:16–17, NIV)

BIBLE STUDY QUESTIONS

Genesis 1; 3:1–24; Luke 4:1–13; Revelation 22:1–5, 12–19

The majestic sweep of the Bible begins with creation in Genesis and is consummated with the re-creation of the world in Revelation. Central to the message of the Bible is what we do wrong and what God does to make it right. Please read Genesis 1.

1. When God created the world (v. 1), it was formless and empty (v. 2). In days 1–3 God gives the world form (light, sky, and earth). In days 4–6 God fills the world (luminaries, birds, fish, and land with animals, including humans). What insights about God and his world can you glean from this simple summary/overview?

_____

_____

_____

_____

2. Since Adam and Eve were made in the image of God (vv. 26–30), what might we learn about God from reflecting on the responsibility given to humans? What do we learn about humans by reflecting on the character and actions of God recorded in Genesis 1?

3. God declares the world good and takes pleasure in it (v. 31). What goodness and pleasure do you especially enjoy—being God's creation and placed in his world?

   GOD WANTS US TO TRUST HIM AND HIS WORD.

4. Read Genesis 3:1–24. The goodness of God's world is polluted and the image of God is fractured when Adam and Eve believe the lie of the serpent and disregard God. What do the serpent's statements imply about the character of God?

   GOD IS A HOLY GOD

5. The consequences of believing Satan rather than trusting God are immediate as God's creation fractures and twists (vv. 7–24). List or discuss a few ways you see and experience God's good world as fractured, distorted, and painful.

    MEN SEEK THEIR SELFISH DESIRES.

6. In the midst of the curses that result from Adam and Eve's rebellion against God, we find the first sign of God's plan of redemption in Genesis 3:15. What is prophesied and how is this fulfilled in the New Testament? (See Rom. 16:20; Heb. 2:14.)

7. The choice of Noah and the call of Abraham are steps in God's restoration process that leads directly to Jesus, who finally and faithfully bears the image of God—humanly and perfectly. What do you learn about Jesus, the Son of God and Son of Adam, as Jesus experiences the temptation of Satan? (Luke 4:1–13)

    YOU SHALL NOT TEMPT THE LORD

8. Read Revelation 22:1–5. The last chapters of the book of Revelation allow us to look at the consummation of God's creating work as God renews, restores, and re-creates the world. What does the renewed world include, and what is it like?

No PAIN, NO DEATH, NO DECEPTION. NO WORRIES.

9. Projecting your life into God's future, how would your life be/feel different if you didn't fear darkness, didn't struggle with sin or other problems of body, mind, and soul, had all the food you wanted, and had direct and immediate access to God?

iT WOULD BE PARADISE. iT iS DIFFICULT TO FATHOM.

10. The renewed creation is the work of God and dependent on the return of Christ (Rev. 22:12–19). How are you supposed to live in the meantime?

WE ARE TO PRESS ON TOWARD OUR HEAVENLY GOAL. WE ARE TO CHRIST'S AMBASSADORS

CHAPTER 2 – GOD'S STORY OF REDEMPTION

GROUP DISCUSSION QUESTIONS

1. How is God's story of redemption structured from a literary point of view? What are the scenes or major chapters of the story? Who are the main characters? The villain? The hero?

   THE GARDEN OF EDEN. THE SNAKE AND THE WOMAN
   ARE THE VILLANS

2. What does God's story of redemption tell you about God? Elaborate.

   GOD IS A GOD OF LOVE. HE DID NOT GIVE UP
   ON A SINFUL MANKIND

3. How does an understanding of God's Story of Redemption affect the way that you live your life? How should it affect the way you live?

4. How would you share the story of God's redemption in an elevator talk (1 minute) so that someone was able to get the basic gist of the story?

5. What would be some effective ways to communicate God's story of redemption to our society, our family, our church?

   LIVE YOUR LIFE AS A WITNESS TO
   CHRIST'S LOVE, LET YOUR LIGHT & SHINE
   SHINE

6. What are some of the stories in the world competing against God's story? What do those stories offer to people? How would you compare them to God's story of redemption?

    THE BIG BANG THEORY

7. Why do you think God's story of redemption resonates so strongly within the human heart?

    MAN SEEKS GOD

8. How are you going to share the story of God's redemption with others in the days to come?

CHAPTER 3

SPEAKER & AUTHOR BIO: RANDY NEWMAN

TEACHING FELLOW, C.S. LEWIS IN-STITUTE – Randy Newman has been with the staff of Cru since 1980 and currently serves with Faculty Commons, their ministry to university professors. He ministers on campuses and elsewhere in our nation's capital to students, professors, and policy shapers. He is an honors graduate from Temple University and has a Masters of Divinity degree from Trinity Evangelical Divinity School, where he is also engaged in doctoral studies. Randy is a Jewish Believer in Jesus and is the former editor of *The Messiah-On-Campus Bulletin*. He lives in Annandale, Virginia, with his wife Pam. He is the author of numerous articles and the books *Questioning Evangelism: Engaging People's Hearts the Way Jesus Did* and *Corner Conversations: Engaging Dialogues about God and Life*, both published by Kregel Publications, and *Bringing the Gospel Home: Witnessing to Family Members, Close Friends, and Others Who Know You Well*, forthcoming from Crossway.

UNDERSTANDING SALVATION

The converted slave trader, John Newton, wrote a song with these words, "Amazing Grace, how sweet the sound, that saved a wretch like me. I once was lost, but now am found, was blind, but now I see." Those words have reverberated around the world as Newton's description of God's salvation of sinners, the likes of us, and have touched the hearts of many. And yet, there is more. If we mine the Scriptures, we will find an even richer understanding of the meaning and depth of our salvation through our Savior Jesus Christ. It is easy, however, in the day-to-day activities of life to lose our sense of wonder and excitement over all that God has done to save us. The purpose of this study is to reignite that enthusiasm for God's gift of salvation and inspire us to give thanks daily to the God who saves.

CHAPTER 3 – UNDERSTANDING SALVATION

The Christian faith engages both the heart and the mind. Thus the goal of the C.S. Lewis Institute, "discipleship of the heart and mind," reflects what God would have for all his people: that they would love him with all their heart, soul, strength, and mind. This calls for a bit of reflection in light of our world's contrasting view of spirituality. Many think the way to "god" is through an emotional or vaguely spiritual experience with little or no thinking involved. Others exalt the mind so far as to reduce the ultimate goal of life to mere intellectual prowess.

The Christian worldview values both mind and heart, seeing them as integrated rather than in competition. The Bible challenges us to understand, consider, know, and meditate upon truth as well as love, feel, taste, experience, and practice godliness. In fact, it is safe to say that the goal of godly living is impossible without rigorous thinking. To the extent that we understand our salvation, we are more likely to experience it.

The purpose of this article is to stimulate thinking *and* doing, reflection *and* obedience. We will examine what God's Word says about our salvation and consider how those truths might work themselves out in our experience.

We could center our study on many different passages from the Bible. We'll choose Paul's prayer for the Ephesians and his introduction to the letter. Consider the first of the two passages:

> *For this reason I kneel before the Father, from whom his whole family in heaven and on earth derives its name. I pray that out of his glorious riches he may strengthen you with power through his Spirit in your inner being, so that Christ may dwell in your hearts through faith. And I pray that you, being rooted and established in love, may have power, together with all the saints, to grasp how wide and long and high and deep is the love of Christ, and to know this love that surpasses knowledge—that you may be filled to the measure of all the fullness of God. (Eph. 3:14–19)*[1]

To "grasp how wide and long and high and deep is the love of Christ" is to understand our salvation. What follows is a reflection or meditation upon this prayer. It will not be as technical or intellectually deep as what you might find in a commentary[2] but more in-depth than what you might find in a brief devotional.[3]

Note first where this prayer occurs in the book of Ephesians. It serves as a hinge between a doctrinally rich description of many things that are true about us, now that we are Christians, and a section on practical Christian living. "For this reason" in verse 14 looks back on all that has been listed about our salvation in chapters 1 and 2. But this prayer also paves the way for all the commands listed and elaborated upon in chapters 4–6.

This pattern (doctrine followed by practice) is typical of Paul's understanding of the Christian life. Who we are, in Christ, sets the stage for how we should live. Or, to be more concise, being

precedes doing. The fact that we are already declared to be chosen to be holy (see Eph. 1:4) paves the way for us to "live a life worthy of the calling" we have (see Eph. 4:1). This reverses the order of most other worldviews that say we should do in order to be. Other religions offer this kind of pattern: if you do this and this and this, you will be fulfilled or holy or enlightened. The gospel offers this instead: because you already are declared to be holy, because of Christ's death on your behalf, you should now *do* things and obey commands *out of response* to your new identity.

If you want to use technical terms, you could say that other religions put the imperative (commands) before the indicative. Christianity puts the indicative before the imperative. The former motivates by obligation. The latter motivates from gratitude. Other religions require you to earn salvation. Christianity offers salvation based on what has already been earned by Christ on your behalf. The difference is monumental.

Second, note how this prayer weaves together the heart and mind. Paul prays (and thus we pray for ourselves and other Christians) that both our intellect and will become engaged. We are to "know" some things as well as be "strengthened." We are to "grasp" and "be filled." Paul reminds us that we already are "rooted and established in love" while praying that we will experience "strength" and "power."

This prayer (3:14–19) echoes Paul's prayer earlier in Ephesians (1:15–21), where he asks God to "enlighten" the "eyes of your heart" so that you/we may "know" several things. This is predominately, although not entirely, an intellectual matter. But that same prayer points to an experience of "power." This is primarily, although not exclusively, an encounter of our entire being, not just our intellect. Again, we see that to understand our salvation is to be transformed by it.

Consider the many "spiritual blessings" enumerated in the introduction to Ephesians (1:3–14):

> *Praise be to the God and Father of our Lord Jesus Christ, who has blessed us in the heavenly realms with every spiritual blessing in Christ. For he chose us in him before the creation of the world to be holy and blameless in his sight. In love he predestined us to be adopted as his sons through Jesus Christ, in accordance with his pleasure and will—to the praise of his glorious grace, which he has freely given us in the One he loves. In him we have redemption through his blood, the forgiveness of sins, in accordance with the riches of God's grace that he lavished on us with all wisdom and understanding. And he made known to us the mystery of his will according to his good pleasure, which he purposed in Christ, to be put into effect when the times will have reached their fulfillment—to bring all things in heaven and on earth together under one head, even Christ.*

In him we were also chosen, having been predestined according to the plan of him who works out everything in conformity with the purpose of his will, in order that we, who were the first to hope in Christ, might be for the praise of his glory. And you also were included in Christ when you heard the word of truth, the gospel of your salvation. Having believed, you were marked in him with a seal, the promised Holy Spirit, who is a deposit guaranteeing our inheritance until the redemption of those who are God's possession—to the praise of his glory.

In this remarkably packed statement, we see mind-boggling components of our salvation:

- We are blessed with every spiritual blessing in Christ.
- We were chosen before the creation of the world to be holy and blameless before him.
- God predestined us to be adopted as his sons.
- We have redemption through Christ's blood.
- We have forgiveness for our trespasses.
- God has lavished his grace upon us.
- God has revealed mysteries to us.
- We have been sealed with the Holy Spirit.

And so much more. Take some time to list other blessings you see in this passage and reflect on what they mean.

Here are just a few sample reflections to model how your meditations on these beautiful truths can transform your life.

Because I have been blessed with every *spiritual* blessing, I can count on God to take care of all my other needs. If he's solved my most urgent eternal problem, alienation from him because of my sin, then I can trust him for temporal material needs such as finances, opportunities, and medical challenges.

Because God chose me before the creation of the world, I can rest in his timelessness. Nothing surprises him. There are no accidents or mistakes in his plan. Even setbacks (major ones, like a serious health challenge, or the most annoying of minor ones, like a flat tire) have a divine imprint upon them, being used by a good God to make me more and more like his Son.

Because God's saving design for me is to be holy and blameless, I can say no to temptations that can compromise my identity as a child of God or bring shame upon the name of Christ or mar my ability to love God wholeheartedly. I can see immorality for what it truly is, an attack against God's character and a poison for my soul, even if my surrounding culture laughs about it, approves of it, or promotes it as something good.

Because God predestined me (yes, I know this is controversial; I'll leave it to you to sort this out on your own[4]), I can see that my salvation is not something I manufactured or earned. I can also extend grace and patience to those around me who don't seem to care about God. Did I come to this place of faith because I was so smart or clever? No, God woke me from my slumber ("dead in your transgressions and sins" is the way Paul describes it in Eph. 2:1). A proud Christian is the ultimate contradiction.

Because I've been adopted, I have privileges and access to God as my father. I can come to him with any and all needs. I don't have to view myself as a second-class citizen in his kingdom. I am a son. (Both men and women should explore the unique term *son* in the New Testament vocabulary. To change this word to *child* does lose something of the special privileges of sonship that the Bible teaches.)

Because I have redemption, I can rejoice that the purposes for which I was originally created can now be experienced. Redemption is a difficult concept for our democratic culture to grasp. There were economic and military realities in New Testament times that, once understood, can illumine our consideration of this term. Sometimes a slave was "redeemed" out of his economic servitude or military status as a prisoner of war so that he could experience freedom. The most graphic depiction of redemption in the Bible occurs in the story of Hosea's wife, Gomer. As an unfaithful wife, Gomer slept around with various men, bringing shame and humiliation upon her husband, children, and herself. Ultimately she was discarded by all her "lovers" and offered up as a slave on the auction block. Who should choose to purchase her after everyone else wanted nothing to do with her? Hosea, her husband! He bought her out of bondage and took her back, so she could fulfill the purposes for which she was created—to be a faithful, loving, accepted, and clean wife. To experience redemption means to be bought back and brought back to the position and purpose for which you were created. When we are redeemed in Christ, even though we once played the whore and worshiped all sorts of other gods, we can now be declared clean, part of the bride of Christ, and return home to the place where we worship the true God. This is what we were made for. This is what we were remade to do and be.

Because we have forgiveness for our trespasses, we don't need to try to balance the books with our good works. We don't need to pursue some system of having our good deeds outweigh our bad deeds. (Is that even possible? Are all deeds weighted the same? Could a good deed of giving money to the poor outweigh an outburst of anger? Could such things really appear on some balance sheet in any kind of meaningful way? Or is this entire system absurd?) Instead, I see all of my sins nailed to the cross. That's why I have forgiveness! It's not based on any deeds I have done. My forgiveness is all based on that one, unspeakably marvelous deed of Christ.

Because my forgiveness flows out of "the riches of God's grace," I can rejoice that it's limitless. In fact, God has "lavished" his grace upon me. The well of forgiveness will never run dry. There will never come a point when I confess a sin to God, and he says, "That's it! No more! I can't forgive that same sin again. You've pushed me past my limit." No sin, no matter how severe or frequent, falls outside the realm of God's forgiving grace.

Because God has made known to me the mystery of his will (specifically, that aspect of his will "which he purposed in Christ"), I can make sense of some things that might otherwise seem confusing. While I might not understand everything and I certainly won't like everything I see happening in the world, I can grasp why some terrible things happen. People are in rebellion against God and have fallen for the devil's schemes. I can understand why I have cravings for sin that I know are evil. I still am drawn to the devil's influence because of my flesh and his dominion as "the prince of the power of the air" (Eph. 2:2, KJV). But I can recognize all this because God has granted me insight to the spiritual realm. His grace, which has been lavished upon me, comes along with "all wisdom and understanding."

Because I have been sealed with the Holy Spirit, I can rest in confidence that nothing can snatch me out of God's hand. I can look within and find God's power at work in my life. This gives me hope, because the Holy Spirit is a down payment and a guarantee of the ultimate total redemption I will experience when I get to heaven. At this point in time, I have but a taste of my ultimate glorification. Every time I experience victory over a sin that tempts me or feel overwhelmed with gratitude for God's blessings or rejoice in praise for who God is, it's like an appetizer of a meal I will one day enjoy in Christ's presence where there will be no temptation or sin or sorrow. Hope for the future flows from the Holy Spirit's work in my life today.

Because Paul describes so many of these blessings with the terms *in Christ* or *with Christ*, I can see all of my life through that lens. The only reason I have a right standing before God or any blessing, for that matter, is because of Christ and his atoning death for me. I can take credit for none of it. I can look at every blessing in my life, from the most dire (deliverance from God's wrath) to the most mundane (daily bread) and respond with "Thanks be to God."

In conclusion, let us reflect on the multifaceted dimensions of our salvation. It obviously centers upon our right standing before a holy, righteous God. Our salvation reflects both his holiness and his love, because he saved us while we were still sinners. Our salvation also penetrates within us and changes us from the inside out. It also overflows into our relationships with others. And it connects us to our temporal world in redemptive ways as well as to the eternal realities where God is glorified endlessly. Understanding our salvation is of utmost importance in the here and now and will continue with increasing joy forever and ever.

NOTES

[1] Unless otherwise noted, all Scripture quotations are from the *New International Version*, 1984.

[2] Reading a commentary on this and other passages is highly recommended as part of the process of "discipleship of heart and mind." Two helpful resources are Peter T. O'Brien, *The Letter to the Ephesians* in The Pillar New Testament Commentary series; and John R.W. Stott, *The Message of Ephesians* in The Bible Speaks Today series.

[3] One very helpful devotional to give you a good overview of the entire Bible is D.A. Carson, *For the Love of God* (Wheaton, IL: Crossway, 1998).

[4] A helpful resource might be J.I. Packer, *Evangelism and the Sovereignty of God* (Downers Grove, IL: InterVarsity Press, 2008).

SCRIPTURE MEMORY VERSE

For it is by grace you have been saved, through faith—and this is not from yourselves, it is the gift of God—not by works, so that no one can boast. (Ephesians 2:8–9, NIV)

BIBLE STUDY QUESTIONS

Ephesians 2:1–10

God saves! In one concise passage the apostle Paul draws together essential elements of the theme of salvation that is present on every page of the Bible. Please read Ephesians 2:1–10.

1. Prior to our new life in Christ, death, paradoxically, is the state in which we live. What are the elements of spiritual death (vv. 1–3)?

   SEPARATION FROM A HOLY GOD

2. By nature humans are "dead in transgressions and sins"—which means that humans are both rebels and failures and therefore under God's wrath. If you could enter a conversation with the apostle, would you readily agree with this statement or would you want to discuss it further? How and why?

Yes I agree

3. Reread verses 1–3 slowly and picture yourself in each line of the verses. What does it look like to be spiritually dead?

Disobedient. We were subject to God's anger

4. Traditionally it has been said that the Christian has three enemies, the world,[1] the flesh,[2] and the devil; all three are referenced in these verses. List or discuss a few ways you see these three deathly enemies active in your life and in the world around you.

Love of material things. Jelousy. covetness

---

1. *The world* is a reference to human culture organized and conducted in a way that excludes God.
2. *The flesh* is a reference to the human psyche organized and constructed in a way that excludes God.

5. Compare and contrast verses 1–3 and 4–6, noting the differences between being spiritually dead and spiritually alive.

_____

_____

_____

_____

6. What is God's motivation and Christ's role in moving us from death to life (vv. 4–10)?

    - God abounds in love

_____

_____

_____

7. Reread verses 4–10 slowly. Imagine God reaching down and bringing you from lying dead in a coffin to active life. What is changing as you receive and embrace life?

_____

_____

_____

_____

8. What is God's role and what is the human role in moving from death to life?

_____

_____

_____

_____

9. *Faith! Christ! Grace!* are words that came alive to the leaders of the revival and renewal of the church during the Reformation. What light does this passage bring to their enthusiastic emphases?

_____

_____

_____

_____

10. Verse 10 could be paraphrased as "Christians are God's works of art created in Christ to accomplish good deeds that God wants us to do." How might this statement enrich and expand your understanding of salvation?

_____

_____

_____

_____

GROUP DISCUSSION QUESTIONS

1. The apostle Paul writes in Ephesians 2:8–9 that we have been "saved by grace through faith alone." Unpack the meaning of this phrase. What is grace? What is faith? What role did God play in our salvation?

    _____

    _____

2. When you blow it and fall into sin again, how does the biblical understanding of repentance, God's grace, and forgiveness help you?

    _____

    _____

3. How does the biblical understanding of salvation affect the way in which you live in society, within your family and in the church?

    _____

    _____

4. How does this understanding of salvation differ from all other religions or worldviews?

    _____

    _____

5. What are some of the metaphors and descriptors used in Scripture to give us a better understanding of our salvation in Christ? Elaborate on their meaning.

    _____

    _____

6. What are some of the blessings that you receive through salvation in Jesus Christ? How do these blessings change the way you live your life?

_____

_____

7. What are some habits that you can practice to help remind yourself of God's amazing grace and his gift of salvation in Christ?

_____

_____

8. In one minute, how would you share your understanding of salvation with someone else? Spend some time later this week writing out your understanding of salvation in more depth.

_____

_____

CHAPTER 4

SPEAKER BIO:
JOEL S. WOODRUFF, ED.D.

VICE PRESIDENT OF DISCIPLESHIP &
OUTREACH, C.S. LEWIS INSTITUTE –
Joel Woodruff has worked in higher education,
"tent-making," nonprofit administration, and
pastoral ministries in Alaska, Israel, Hungary,
France, and Northern Virginia. He served as
Dean of Students, Chaplain, and Professor of
Bible & Theology at European Bible Institute,
where he helped train Europeans both for professional ministry and to be Christian leaders
in the marketplace. Prior to joining the C.S.
Lewis Institute, he was on the leadership team
of Oakwood Services International, a nonprofit educational and humanitarian organization.
He is a graduate of Wheaton College, earned
his M.Div. from Gordon-Conwell Theological Seminary, and has a doctorate in Organizational Leadership from Nova Southeastern
University. As a Parish-Pulpit Fellow, he studied Biblical Backgrounds & Archaeology in
Israel for a year.

AUTHOR BIO:
STEPHEN EYRE, M.DIV.

DIRECTOR, C.S. LEWIS INSTITUTE
- CINCINNATI – Stephen Eyre has served
both in college campus ministry and pastoral
ministry for more than twenty years. He has
written numerous books, Bible study guides,
and devotional books that have been published
nationally and internationally through Inter-
Varsity Press, Zondervan, and Victor Press.
Stephen has written several study guides for
C.S. Lewis Institute publications including
Mere Christianity, Screwtape Letters, and *Let-
ters to Malcolm; Chiefly on Prayer,* as well as
the Bible Study Questions for this publication.
He earned a B.A. in history from Clearwater
Christian College and a M.Div. from Covenant
Theological Seminary.

GOD'S PLAN FOR OUR GROWTH

When a person is born again by confessing his sin and putting his faith in Jesus Christ, he becomes a child of God. But God's work in that person's life doesn't stop there. He wants that child to grow into a mature disciple of Jesus Christ who looks more like Jesus in his thoughts, words, and deeds every day. Recent studies have shown that many in the church today are not growing into spiritual adults, but rather continue to live as spiritual infants — still stuck in the lifestyle and morality of the secular world around them. They are not experiencing the joy and fullness of life that comes from living a life of holiness and obedience in dedication to their Savior Jesus Christ. The Bible uses two terms to help us understand our position in Christ — justification and sanctification. An understanding of these two important words will help us understand God's plan for our growth. For the Lord's desire is that we know who we are, sinners who have been justified by Christ, and that we know our potential, saints who are living holy lives that honor and glorify God.

The human race has a character flaw: sin. We have a "sinful nature," referred to in the Greek as *sarx*: in older translations it is rendered as "the flesh." The Bible portrays us as spiritually and genetically addicted to sin. It is a virus that infects everything. Whatever sin infects turns terminally malignant. Sin is a power that addicts, infects, enslaves, and destroys.

The presence, actions, and power of sin are described by the apostle Paul in the context of his own character struggle.

> *When I want to do good, evil is right there with me. For in my inner being I delight in God's law; but I see another law at work in the members of my body, waging war against the law of my mind and making me a prisoner of the law of sin at work within my members. What a wretched man I am! Who will rescue me from this body of death? (Rom. 7:21–24)[1]*

The answer to Paul's desperate plea, *who will rescue me from slavery to sin?* is God.

Salvation is the comprehensive term we use to describe God's rescue. We have terms to expound and explain the process of God's rescue; two of these are *justification* and *sanctification.* *Justification* is what God does for us, and sanctification addresses what we must do in response. By means of justification and sanctification, we are empowered to fight the battle of sin and be enriched by God's blessings.

JUSTIFICATION

Briefly, justification can be defined as God's saving actions in Christ applied to sin-infected beings. *Justification* is a rich and complex term that needs to be unpacked. We will look at it from two different angles: the blood of Christ and spiritual union with Christ.

The Blood of Christ
> *All have sinned and fall short of the glory of God, and are justified freely by his grace through the redemption that came by Christ Jesus. God presented him as a sacrifice of atonement, through faith in his blood. (Rom. 3:23–25)*

I used addiction and infection as metaphors to introduce the need for justification. But there are other helpful ways to think about the sin problem. In the preceding verses the apostle Paul used three:

Just as if I never sinned

Justified is a legal term taken from the courts. To be justified means that the accused is declared innocent of the charges—not guilty. The prisoner is released and given a clean record.

Redemption is a term taken from the slave markets. To be redeemed means that someone paid off the slave master, and the slave is now a freed person.

Propitiation is a Greek word, translated in the *New International Version* as *sacrifice of atonement.* The word is taken from the temple system. The consequences for failing to keep the stipulations of the covenant fall on the substitutionary sacrifice; the worshiper is pronounced clean and is reconciled to God.

Putting together these three images, justification means that an amazing change has taken place: the sinner is no longer guilty of sin; the slave is no longer a slave; the covenant breaker is no longer estranged from God.

Justification means that there is a change of status: from guilty to not guilty, from slave to free, from foul to clean. This change of status takes place by means of the blood of Christ. The centrality of the death of Christ is in view when we speak of the "cross of Christ."

There is something mystical in the blood of Christ, some spiritual power at work. Sin is fatal. No one gets out of this world alive. For reasons that we can barely glimpse, Christ's death is an acceptable substitute to God for the consequences of our sin; his death unleashes spiritual, transforming power.

Gospel-hymn writers of earlier centuries embraced the blood of Christ in ways that can seem strange to twenty-first-century moderns.

What can wash away my sin? Nothing but the blood of Jesus. (Robert Lowry)

There is power, power, wonder-working power, in the blood of the Lamb. (L.E. Jones)

There is a fountain filled with blood, drawn from Immanuel's veins. (William Cowper)

Living in a world preoccupied with the dimension of the physical makes it hard for us to grasp such a spiritual power available by means of the blood of Christ. To really embrace the wonder of Christ's blood that produced justification, we need the broader rationality that allows us to take out all the pieces in the puzzle box, not just the ones that are acceptable to a materialistic and rationalistic age.

CHAPTER 4 – GOD'S PLAN FOR OUR GROWTH

C.S. Lewis, in *The Lion, the Witch and the Wardrobe*, used the death of Aslan to portray the mysterious power of the blood of Christ. Aslan dies in the place of the traitor, Edmund. Susan and Lucy are filled with grief. They are shocked and thrilled when they discover Aslan alive the next morning. Aslan explains:

> "It means," said Aslan, "that though the Witch knew the Deep Magic, there is a magic still deeper which she did not know. Her knowledge goes back only to the dawn of time. But if she could have looked a little further back...before Time dawned, she would have read there a different incantation. She would have known that when a willing victim who had committed no treachery was killed in a traitor's stead, the Table would crack and Death itself would start working backwards."[2]

The power of justification is activated by faith. We must believe it. Martin Luther unleashed the Reformation because the teaching of justification by faith captured his heart. He understood that no power on earth, not even good intentions and good works, was enough to save us from sin. Faith was the power that opened the soul's door to receive salvation. Luther said:

> Faith is God's work in us that changes us and gives new birth from God (John 1:13). It kills the Old Adam and makes us completely different people. It changes our hearts, our spirits, our thoughts and all our powers. It brings the Holy Spirit with it. Yes, it is a living, creative, active and powerful thing, this faith.

> Faith is a living, bold trust in God's grace, so certain of God's favor that it would risk death a thousand times trusting in it. Such confidence and knowledge of God's grace makes you happy, joyful and bold in your relationship to God and all creatures.[3]

Faith in the justifying blood of Christ changes our status and has soul-shaping power. Peter Haile, in his little classic on the Christian faith, *The Difference God Makes*, writes of a friend who was feeling out of touch with God and consequently upset, disturbed, and edgy.

> "But aren't believers promised joy and peace?" I stopped him and said, "Yes, Believers are promised joy and peace..." It was his failure to take God at his Word, to act on the assumption that God really means what he says–that was the trouble.[4]

Faith not only receives but unleashes God's saving power. In a discussion about spirituality and mental health, a doctor at a psychiatric institution commented, "Half the people in here could walk out today if they could believe that they were forgiven."

Spiritual Union with Christ

But really, how is it that what Jesus Christ did two thousand years ago makes a difference today? In *Mere Christianity* (Book 4) C.S. Lewis notes that we have to have a new view of time to make sense of Christianity. The Greek word *chronos* refers to time as a succession of moments. The Greeks had another word for time that is more than a succession of moments: chairos is an eternal view that transcends the moment. A graphic can help us see this.

MODERN TIME: CHRONOS
Separated by a series of moments

In contrast to a series of moments by which we are increasingly removed from the original event, we have biblical time in which we are not separated but have an immediate connection with that which precedes us, no matter how long ago the event may have taken place.

ETERNITY
Not separated by a series of moments

The New Testament writers understood that it was possible to be "in Christ" and for Christ to be in us in a way that leaps over the moments. It is this eternal time and spiritual connection that makes Christ's blood work for us. When we view time in this way, we have a true and immediate connection of Christ

Although he was not present at Christ's crucifixion, the apostle Paul can say:

> *I have been crucified with Christ and I no longer live, but Christ lives in me. The life I live in the body, I live by faith in the Son of God, who loved me and gave himself for me. (Gal. 2:20)*

In these words we have spiritual participation in the person and work of Christ that is not restricted by time or by space. This way of seeing life in Christ is pervasive in the New Testament. Consider:

> *Therefore, if anyone is in Christ, he is a new creation; the old has gone, the new has come! (2 Cor. 5:17)*

> *If we have been united with him like this in his death, we will certainly also be united with him in his resurrection. (Rom. 6:5)*

Believers are in Christ and with Christ in all that has happened to him.

> *God, who is rich in mercy, made us alive with Christ even when we were dead in transgressions ... And God raised us up with Christ and seated us with him in the heavenly realms in Christ Jesus. (Eph. 2:4–6)*

The mystical union was at the heart of the teaching of the great Reformer John Calvin.

> First, we must understand that as long as Christ remains outside of us, and we are separated from him, all that he has suffered and done for the salvation of the human race remains useless and of no value for us. Therefore, to share with us what he has received from the Father, he had to become ours and to dwell with us.[5]

"In Christ" is a mystical/spiritual union that becomes a believer's new identity. Origen, a teacher in the early church, wrote, "He became what we are that we might become like he is." Because Jesus died to sin, those who believe in him have died to sin as well. Because Jesus has been raised from the dead, we are raised from the dead. Because God has raised Christ to the heavenly realms and seated him at his right hand, we too have been raised to the heavenlies and are seated at God's right hand.

As a result of our mystical union with Christ, my identity is now that of Christ; this means I am justified and no longer guilty of sin, no longer estranged from God, no longer a slave to spiritual forces that would overpower and deform me.

SANCTIFICATION

Now that we are justified, we can share in the process of sanctification: growth in holiness and character development.

The apostle Paul's teaching of justification by faith raised questions: "What then? Shall we sin because we are not under law but under grace?" (Rom. 6:15). In other words, "If I am eternally declared 'not guilty' by God, can't I now do anything I want to do?" This of course misses the point. Justification is not about "fire insurance"—believing in Jesus so you won't go to hell; it's about character development.

Sanctification means that we are now free, through the power of the Holy Spirit, to make moral choices that prior to justification we were not able to make. Sanctification means that we now can say no to that which is not good and right and yes to that which is pleasing to God.

> *Therefore do not let sin reign in your mortal body so that you obey its evil desires. Do not offer the parts of your body to sin, as instruments of wickedness, but rather offer yourselves to God, as those who have been brought from death to life; and offer the parts of your body to him as instruments of righteousness. For sin shall not be your master, because you are not under law, but under grace. (Rom. 6:12–14)*

Character requires restraint. Some years ago in a famous study researchers put young children in a room and placed a marshmallow in front of each of them. They were left alone and told not to eat the marshmallow until the researcher returned. If they were able to restrain themselves, they would get the marshmallow and a reward.

Some of the children were able to restrain themselves; others were not. Over the next thirty years the children who participated were tracked. Many of those who were not able to restrain themselves lived in poverty and prisons. Most of those who were able to restrain themselves became professionals and lived what most would describe as successful lives.

Morality of course is about more than restraint. It is about saying no to sin and yes to God. The Greek word for *sanctify* means to "make holy." To become holy means that we grow so close to God that we share in the character of God and live in ways that are pleasing to God.

Good character has "traits," ways of thinking and acting that we can identify. Perhaps the most comprehensive list of character traits listed in the New Testament is the fruit of the Spirit: "love, joy, peace, patience, kindness, goodness, faithfulness, gentleness and self-control" (Gal. 5:22–23).

It is important to note that these traits are indeed the fruit of the Spirit; that is, they are not the result of merely doing one's duty by the exercise of willpower. The fruit of the Spirit is the manifestation of the character of Jesus Christ that grows in our lives as, by faith, we live in him and he lives in us.

A person of good character used to be described as virtuous. A virtuous person is skillful, even artful, in doing good. In his book *After Virtue*, Alistair McIntyre traced the sources of the moral crises of modern culture to the loss of virtue.

For the individual, in *Mere Christianity* (Book 3) C.S. Lewis addressed what sort of behavior God expects of Christians. He explored the four classic virtues and added the three theological virtues; these seven provide a helpful picture of good character: prudence, temperance, justice, fortitude, faith, hope, and love.

Jonathan Edwards, a leader of the First Great Awakening in colonial America, described the character produced by sanctification in his classic *Religious Affections*. "The strength of a good soldier of Jesus Christ appears in nothing more than in steadfastly maintaining the holy calm, meekness, sweetness and benevolence of his mind, amidst all the storms, injuries, strange behavior and surprising acts and events of this evil and unreasonable world."[6]

Sanctification is about the process of becoming holy. Holy people are whole, full, complete, valuable, centered, and strong; they bring God's presence as they bear the image of Christ.

CONCLUSION

One of my sons is a heroin addict. He has been clean for a number of years, but each day brings new challenges; he never takes his sobriety for granted. He lives in Seattle but recently came back home to Cincinnati for a visit. He was careful about whom he called, as he didn't want to be exposed to "friends" who might tempt him. He was also cautious about where he went; he even made sure that he went to bed before he became too stressed and tired. His goal is to live a healthy life, free from the power of addiction. He has been down the road of addiction and knows that it is a dead end. He doesn't want to go that way anymore. His healthy choices and clean life take work; I am proud of him.

Justification and sanctification are the means by which we have been empowered by God to face our sin problem head-on. It's a battle for us too. Our goal should be to live so that God will be proud of us, and one day in the light of heaven we hear the divine accolade, "Well done, good and faithful servant" (Matt. 25:21).

I have come to believe everything we experience is a vehicle for shaping our character. By every choice we make and in every action we take, we are either formed to be more like God's Son, Jesus, or we are being deformed to something less than human.

I close with a sobering proposal by C.S. Lewis:

> It is a serious thing to live in a society of possible gods and goddesses, to remember that the dullest and most uninteresting person you talk to may one day be a creature which, if you saw it now, you would be strongly tempted to worship, or else a horror and a corruption such as you now meet, if at all, only in a nightmare. All day long we are, in some degree, helping each other to one or other of these destinations. It is in the light of these overwhelming possibilities, it is with the awe and the circumspection proper to them, that we should conduct all our dealings with one another, all friendships, all loves, all play, all politics.[7]

NOTES

[1] Unless otherwise noted, Scripture quotations are from the *New International Version*, 1984.

[2] C.S. Lewis, *The Lion, the Witch and the Wardrobe* (1950; repr., New York: Macmillan/Collier, 1970), 159–160.

[3] Martin Luther, *Martin Luther, An Introduction to St. Paul's Letter to the Romans,* trans. by R.E. Smith (1994), Johann K. Irmischer edition of Dr. Martin Luther's *Vermischte Deutsche Schriften*, 1854, Vol. 63, pp 124–125

[4] Peter Haile, *The Difference God Makes (Downers Grove, IL: InterVarsity, 1981), 14.*

[5] John Calvin, *The Institutes of the Christian Religion* III.i.I.

[6] Jonathan Edwards, *Religious Affections* (Carlisle, PA: Banner of Truth Trust, 1986), 278.

[7] C.S. Lewis, *The Weight of Glory*, quoted in C.S. Lewis, *The Joyful Christian: 127 Readings* (New York: Macmillan, 1977), 197.

SCRIPTURE MEMORY VERSE

To the church of God in Corinth, to those sanctified in Christ Jesus and called to be his holy people, together with all those everywhere who call on the name of our Lord Jesus Christ. (1 Corinthians 1:2, NIV)

BIBLE STUDY QUESTIONS

Romans 3:21-31; 8:1–17

Karl Menninger, a renowned psychiatrist, published a book in the 70's titled *Whatever Became of Sin*? From a theologian's perspective, it was not a great book. But the title was right on! Sin is no longer a word we use to describe wrongful behavior. However, God takes sin very seriously. The classic term to describe his initial work of deliverance is *justification*. The classic term to describe the subsequent, resulting freedom and growth is *sanctification*. Please read Romans 3:21–31.

1. Jews tried to follow the Old Testament Law as a means for overcoming sin. What hope does God offer those who know they have failed to become righteous by law?

_____

_____

_____

_____

2. These verses are packed with key phrases that describe God's liberating work. First, we are *justified freely* (v. 24), which means to be legally acquitted of all wrongdoing. What is free and what is costly about our justification?

3. The word *redemption* (v. 24) comes from the slave market and means to be bought from slavery to sin into fellowship with God. How have you experienced deliverance from the slavery of avoiding and disobeying God?

4. The words *sacrifice of atonement* (v. 25) come from the temple sacrifices. How do you respond to the fact that Christ died the horrible death you deserved.

5. Once God has broken the power of sin through justification, he leads into the battle to stay free from sin. What resounding good news does Paul declare to those who struggle with sin (Rom. 8:1–17)?

_____

_____

_____

_____

6. After looking through all these verses, describe how the entire Trinity—Father, Son, and Spirit—is involved in our deliverance?

_____

_____

_____

_____

7. Paul states that Christians do not live according to the sinful nature (v. 4) and are not controlled by the sinful nature (v. 9). How does that fit with your experience? Explain.

_____

_____

_____

_____

8. What role does the mind play in a life of sin or a life of righteousness (vv. 5–8)?

_____

_____

_____

_____

9. In living in true spiritual freedom that created a life pleasing to God, we have an obligation (v. 12). What is our part and what is the Spirit's part in fulfilling that obligation (vv. 12–17)?

_____

_____

_____

_____

10. Considering both passages in this study (Rom. 3:21–31 and Rom. 8:1–17), how do both justification and sanctification, unleashed by faith, bring about the blessing of salvation?

_____

_____

_____

GROUP DISCUSSION QUESTIONS

1. What does it mean to be justified? How has Christ through His redemptive work justified us in God's sight?

   _____

   _____

2. Knowing that you have been justified by Jesus, how does that affect the way in which you live out your daily life?

   _____

   _____

3. How would you respond to the accusation that you can't be justified since you still continue to sin at times?

   _____

   _____

4. What does it mean to be sanctified?

   _____

   _____

5. Knowing that you have been declared to be holy, a saint, how does that affect the way in which you think of yourself? Live out your life?

   _____

   _____

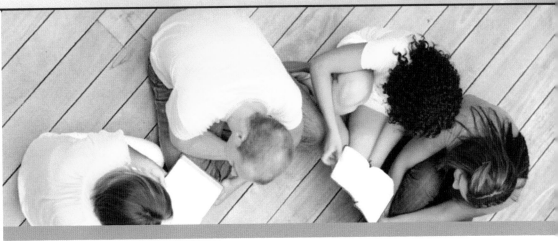

6. How would you respond to the statement, "You're no saint. Saints are holy people who don't sin and do miracles."

_____

_____

7. How would you explain the idea that you are both "already and not yet," a saint?

_____

_____

8. What strategies can you implement in your life to put yourself in a place to grow into a more mature disciple of Jesus Christ?

_____

_____

CHAPTER 5

SPEAKER BIO: THOMAS A. TARRANTS, III, D. MIN.

VICE PRESIDENT OF MINISTRY, C.S. LEWIS INSTITUTE – Tom Tarrants has lived in the Washington D.C. area since 1978 and served as President of the C.S. Lewis Institute from 1998 to April 2010. Prior to coming to the Institute, he served as co-pastor of Christ Our Shepherd Church and Director of The School for Urban Mission, both based in Washington, D.C. He is the author of two books and is a consultant for Church Discipleship Services, developing discipleship programs and materials to strengthen the local church. Tom earned a Master of Divinity Degree from Eastern Mennonite Seminary and Doctor of Ministry from Fuller Theological Seminary.

AUTHOR BIO: WILLIAM L. "BILL" KYNES, PH.D.

SENIOR FELLOW, C.S. LEWIS INSTI-TUTE – Bill Kynes is the senior pastor of Cornerstone Evangelical Free Church, in Annandale, Virginia, where he has served since 1986. He was an undergraduate at the University of Florida with a major in philosophy. There he also played quarterback on the football team and was later inducted into the university's Athletic Hall of Fame. He attended Oxford University as a Rhodes Scholar, receiving an M.A. in theology. He received an M.Div. from Trinity Evangelical Divinity School, in Deerfield, Illinois, before returning to England for a Ph.D. in New Testament from Cambridge University.

THE COST OF DISCIPLESHIP

From the very beginning of his earthly ministry, Jesus told his disciples that following him would be costly. But he also promised you will be blessed "when people insult you, persecute you and falsely say all kinds of evil against you because of me" (Matt. 5:11). Many in the church today have either never read those words, or have tried to ignore them. No one likes to suffer or pay a price for his or her faith. And yet, if we really do have the truth about reality and it is found in Christ, then we must be willing to risk all in order to be faithful to him. The modern Christian martyr Jim Elliot wrote in his journals, "He is no fool who gives what he cannot keep to gain what he cannot lose." The intent of this study is to encourage you to consider the cost of following Jesus and at the same time realize that there really is no better way to live life to the fullest.

CHAPTER 5 – THE COST OF DISCIPLESHIP

Since the U.S. government moved to an all-volunteer military in the 1970's, the army has advertized itself to potential recruits in various ways. In the 1980's the slogan was "Be all that you can be. Join the U.S. Army" or "It's a great place to start." The army provided training that would prepare you for the job market, and through the G.I. Bill you could get help with college tuition. It was a great deal: Do yourself a favor. Fulfill your potential. Be all that you can be. Things were relatively peaceful in those days; being in the army was almost like enrolling in a technical college for four years, with some physical training and discipline thrown in.

But in 1991 when the First Gulf War began, all these new army recruits were suddenly saying, "You mean I have to leave my family and fight a war? You want me to go to the desert? Where in the world is Qatar? Excuse me, but that's not in my contract." But, of course, it was. "Sorry, soldier; you didn't read the small print. You go where we want you to go."

Now the army ads are much different. In fact, they are often addressed more to the parents than to their sons and daughters. In a time of prolonged war, with a deadly combat zone, it is the parents who are the most hesitant about army service. One ad basically says, when your child talks about enlisting, listen before you just say no. Another tries a form of flattery: "You made them strong. We'll make them *army* strong." Things have changed.

As you look at the ministry of Jesus in the Gospels, you see that he was attracting a large army of people who surrounded him wherever he went. They thought that his journey to Jerusalem was a victory march for the crowning of the Messiah. They wanted to be there when he claimed his throne—to bask in his reflected glory and to grab a share of the prize for themselves.

But Jesus didn't want any misunderstanding. There was to be no neglected small print. He wanted to make it quite clear what was required of anyone who would be his disciple and enter the kingdom of God. Consider these words:

> *If anyone comes to me and does not hate his father and mother, his wife and children, his brothers and sisters—yes, even his own life—he cannot be my disciple. And anyone who does not carry his cross and follow me cannot be my disciple. (Luke 14:26)[1]*

Or these:

> *In the same way, any of you who does not give up everything he has cannot be my disciple. (Luke 14:33)*

Jesus is declaring what it means to become his follower, a member of his army. And no one should enlist without fully understanding what it demands and without first counting the cost (cf. Luke 14:28–32). From the beginning Jesus is entirely upfront and honest. This is an all-or-nothing proposition. You must follow me completely or not at all. In contrast to your commitment to me, you must hate your father and mother, your wife and children.

Undoubtedly these are harsh words, especially when we give so much attention to the value of marriage and family relationships. We may blunt the sharpness of Jesus' words a bit when he talks of *hating* one's family members. We point out that the Semitic mind moved in contrasts and extremes—light and darkness, truth and falsehood, love and hate—primary colors with no shades of gray. And in fact, Jesus himself *loved* his own mother, making sure that she would be cared for even as he was dying on the cross (John 19:25–27). Surely, we're not to *hate* our parents. Jesus is just talking about loving him *more*, we say, and that's true. And of course Jesus wasn't literally saying that every one of his followers must be crucified just as he was or that every one must actually give away all his possessions.

But clearly Jesus is saying that to be his disciple a person must put him in first place among all one's relational loyalties. Any one of you who is not fully devoted to me, he says, anyone who does not give up his claim of ownership on everything he has and even his own life cannot be my disciple.

Immediately, you have to ask yourself, what sort of person makes this kind of demand? If I demanded such a commitment, you'd think I was crazy—or at least you should. To make such a demand, Jesus can't be merely a religious wise man—a mere teacher—sharing a few pearls of wisdom about how best to get along in the world. Not even a holy prophet could say the kinds of things Jesus says here. A prophet says, Follow the ways of God; Jesus says, Follow *me*—supremely.

If we would be his disciples, Jesus demands our ultimate and absolute devotion—the kind of devotion that rightly belongs to God alone. If Jesus is not divine, we must say he was demented if not downright demonic in making these demands, something along the lines of a Jim-Jones-like cult leader.

Do you want to be a Christian, a follower, a disciple of Jesus Christ (and these are all ways of saying the same thing)? Then consider again his words—"If anyone comes to me and does not hate his father and mother, his wife and children, his brothers and sisters—yes, even his own life—he cannot be my disciple. And anyone who does not carry his cross and follow me cannot be my disciple ... In the same way, any of you who does not give up everything he has cannot be my disciple."

Unreasonable Demands?

These are hard words, and many see these demands as entirely unreasonable, impossible, and unthinkable. But let me try to put them in another light. I am a pastor, and as a pastor I perform weddings. And as one who officiates at weddings, I am struck by the fact that these requirements of Jesus sound strangely similar to what is expected in a marriage. Isn't the commitment made in a marriage just as exclusive, as unconditional, and as demanding as what Jesus set before us?

I say to the groom, "Will you have this woman to be your wedded wife? ... Will you love her, comfort her, honor, and keep her for better, for worse, for richer, for poorer in sickness and in health; to love and to cherish and forsaking all others, keep you only unto her, so long as you both shall live?" And of course I ask the same thing of the bride. And each of them will say to the other, "With this ring I thee wed and with all my worldly goods I thee endow ..." And doesn't Paul instruct husbands to love their wives just as Christ loved the church and gave himself up for her—unto death?"

Isn't all this included in the words, "Will you marry me?" That is, "Will you make me the pre-eminent person in your life? Will you set aside your parents, your brothers and sisters, and all your other friends, and devote yourself first and foremost to me? Will you give up sole ownership of all that you own and share with me all that you have, as I make the same commitment to you?"

Those are incredible requests, yet that's what marriage entails—no other lovers on the side, no secret bank accounts, no higher loyalties—none. That's what marriage means—or at least it ought to.

And certainly this points to one of the purposes of premarital counseling—to spell out what this commitment in marriage looks like. I want couples to read the small print, so that they can go beyond the romantic thrill associated with getting married and face up to the challenge, the commitment, and the devotion that marriage requires. Those who are getting married must first count the cost. I don't want any husband or wife I marry to be able to say at some later point when the harsh winds of hardship blow, "That's not in my contract!" For it is in your contract. Marriage demands everything of you. That's what you sign up for—nothing less.

It's a funny thing though. Even when they understand the unconditional contract of marriage, people still *want* to get married. In fact, they *delight* to get married. Why is that? Because there is something so attractive about their husband- or wife-to-be that they are drawn almost irresistibly to give of themselves to that person in love. They long to enter into that exclusive, intimate, loving relationship which marriage represents. They dream of the joy that marriage can bring. They long to entrust themselves to the other, for they believe that their marriage partner can be trusted with their very lives. So they do it.

People who are getting married don't think of what they're *giving up*; they think only of what they are *gaining*. They don't think of it as some great sacrifice to be made, or some heavy burden to be borne, or some solemn duty to be performed for some greater good. Getting married is a joy; it's a delight; it's a cause for great rejoicing. They want everybody to know about it. A wedding is a public event, something to celebrate with a big party!

Becoming a follower of Jesus Christ must be like that, too. A Christian is one who wants to gain Christ. When you see his character, his truth, his trustworthiness, his overwhelming love and beauty, then you desire him as that precious pearl that is worth everything to obtain. It is with joy that you go and sell all that you have to gain that one precious pearl.

The apostle Paul experienced that. He had an impressive résumé, and much to be proud of, yet he wrote, "But whatever was to my profit I now consider loss for the sake of Christ. What is more, I consider everything a loss compared to the surpassing greatness of knowing Christ Jesus my Lord, for whose sake I have lost all things. I consider them rubbish, that I may gain Christ" (Phil. 3:7–8). Nothing that this world has to offer can compare to this surpassing greatness of knowing of Jesus Christ.

CHAPTER 5 – THE COST OF DISCIPLESHIP

Peter expresses the same excitement. He wrote to the Christian believers of their experience of Christ: "Though you have not seen him, you love him; and even though you do not see him now, you believe in him and are filled with an inexpressible and glorious joy" (1 Pet. 1:8). It is a surpassing greatness, an inexpressible and glorious joy. This is what is offered to the follower of Jesus Christ. To gain Christ is to know a satisfaction, a delight, a deep contentment that this world knows nothing of. It is a present reality with the promise of an eternal reward. And that pearl can be yours; you, too, can be my disciple, Jesus says. Everyone can afford it; all it costs is all that you have.

Do you mean everything, Lord? Yes, everything.

But does that mean, Lord: "mother and father, wife and children"?

He answers, *Yes, even they must be entrusted into my care while you follow me. Will you trust me?* he asks each one of us.

John White, who was associate professor of psychiatry at the University of Manitoba and author of a number of very helpful Christian books, speaks of his own struggle with this demand of discipleship in an extraordinary story from his book, *The Cost of Commitment*. It is worth quoting at length.

Once I had a premonition that my wife and infant son would be killed in a flying accident ... We were to travel separately from the U.S. to Bolivia, South America. She would fly via Brazil, Buenos Aires, then north to Bolivia. I was to visit Mexico, several Central American countries, Venezuela, Colombia and other countries, to strengthen Christian work among students, before joining them in Bolivia.

The premonition came with sickening certainty just before we parted on the night of a wild snowstorm. I felt I was a cowardly fool as I drove away and saw Lorrie silhouetted in the yellow light of the doorway, surrounded by swirling snowflakes. Why didn't I go back and tell her I would cancel the flights? Why didn't I act on this foreboding?

Yet I felt a fool. I didn't believe in premonitions—and she would probably laugh. Besides I was late, I had to get to the place where I would spend the night before my early morning flight. Fear, shame, guilt, nausea, all boiled inside me during the miserable drive to my hotel. No conversation was possible with the man who was driving me.

In bed I tossed in misery. Of course I prayed. By faith I was going to have it licked. Faith? In the presence of so powerful a premonition? My mouth was dry. My limbs shook. God was a million miles away. The hours crawled by, each one a year of fear. Why didn't I get dressed, hire a car and go back to them?

"What's the matter? Can't you trust me?"

I was startled. Was God speaking?

"Yes, I'll trust you—if you promise to give them back to me."

Silence.

Then, "And if I don't promise? If I don't give them back to you, will you stop trusting me?"

Oh God, what are you saying? My heart had stopped and I couldn't breathe.

"Can you not entrust them to me in death as well as in life?"

Suddenly a physical warmth flowed through all my body. I think I wept a little. My words came tremblingly and weakly, "Yes, I place them in your hands. I know you will take care of them, in life or in death."

And my trembling subsided. Peace—better by far than martinis on an empty stomach—flowed over and over me. And drowsily I drifted off to sleep.

Hate them? How could I ever hate them? Yet by faith I had said in effect: I will do your will whatever it costs to me or them, and I will trust you.

Their plane crashed. Everyone on board was killed. But my wife had also had a premonition and cut their journey short, getting off the plane the stop before the tragedy occurred.

I am grateful for the way it worked out. But I didn't know beforehand that things would go as they did. And had it not worked out that way I would have grieved (God knows how I would have grieved), but I would not have regretted my decision to trust and to go forward.

This is what it means to follow Christ fully.[2]

Chapter 5 – The Cost of Discipleship

Pseudomarriage and Pseudodiscipleship

The demands of discipleship are like the demands of marriage. But as we think of marriage, there is a disturbing trend in our country these days. Instead of getting married, many couples are simply living together. The number of unmarried-couple households recorded by the U.S. Census Bureau multiplied almost ten times in the past forty years. And almost two-thirds of the people born between 1963 and 1974 first cohabited, without marrying.[3]

I have to say, cohabiting seems like a very sensible thing to do, and I can understand its attraction. Surely, no one buys a car without first giving it a test drive. Shouldn't we try out living together first before making some big, binding commitment?

And why do we even need to make that kind of commitment anyway? We love each other; isn't that all that counts? And if we no longer love each other, then why should we have to stay together? If someone else comes along who attracts me, why should I have to be locked in to just one partner? Cohabiting allows me to keep my options open; isn't that what it means to be free? Cohabitation before or instead of marriage has now become quite normal.

Yet no matter how normal it becomes, such cohabitation is a form of deception for the simple reason that it is a result of a confusion of categories. You see, cohabitation looks a lot like marriage—you have a man and woman living in the same house together, sharing the same bed. But, in fact, it differs from marriage in the one essential thing that makes a marriage a marriage. Cohabiting couples, I'm sure, share a certain kind of romantic love—but it's a love that's lacking that one essential element that comes in true marital love. It lacks commitment—that public pledge of exclusive, unconditional, lifelong, loyal love that makes the nature of that relationship very clear to everyone affected by it.

That's why cohabiting before marriage isn't a trial marriage at all. It is nothing like a marriage, for it lacks the one thing that makes a marriage a marriage. And the testimony of both the Bible and human history is that the kind of relationship between a man and woman to be had in cohabitation is contrary to how we were created to live. We are so made that our lives as men and women together most flourish, and the society we live in most flourishes, when men and women live in exclusive, committed lifelong relationships of loyal love, recognized publicly through the covenant of marriage.[4]

People who cohabit are deceived into thinking they are experiencing marriage when they're not. It's an imitation, a poor reflection, a shadow of the real thing. They don't know what it is to give of themselves fully and to live with someone who is committed to them with all their heart and soul unconditionally, exclusively, with a love that only death can destroy.

Now let's get back to those hard words of Jesus we've been considering: "If anyone comes to me and does not hate his father and mother, his wife and children, his brothers and sisters—yes, even his own life—he cannot be my disciple. And anyone who does not carry his cross and follow me cannot be my disciple ... In the same way, any of you who does not give up everything he has cannot be my disciple."

Notice carefully the word *cannot* in that phrase. Jesus didn't say that if you don't love him above all else that he wouldn't allow you to be his disciple, as if it were a matter of his giving you his permission. The word here is *dynatai*, which suggests not permission but possibility. In other words, it's not possible to be Jesus' disciple without these conditions. A failure to commit yourself to him exclusively and unconditionally is *incompatible* with what it means to be a follower of Jesus Christ.

Imagine for a moment someone coming to the wedding altar and saying, Yes, I want to get married to you, so long as I can continue to sleep around with other women, and I can just give you ten percent of my income, and I'm free to come and go in this marriage whenever I like.

No, you don't get it, we would say. That's not marriage. That's something else entirely. That's not what marriage means.

Jesus is saying the same thing about being his disciple. It means an exclusive, unconditional, loyal love that is supreme in one's life. To have a relationship with God himself through Jesus Christ is like a marriage; it requires this kind of commitment, in a sense, by *definition*. Without it, there can be no relationship at all. You can have a halfhearted, semicommitted relationship with a pagan god, perhaps, but not with Yahweh, the Lord, the God of the Bible who created the heaven and earth and who has now revealed himself in Jesus Christ. It's just not possible. He is a jealous God; he will tolerate no rivals; you shall have no other gods before him. There is simply no other way to relate to this God.

Do you see what this means? It means that a lot a people are deceived. They think they can engage in spiritual cohabitation, having a kind of spiritual relationship with God without any sort of public and exclusive commitment. They think they can have a relationship on their own private terms, when they want it, however it suits them, without that unconditional and exclusive commitment to Christ.

Superficially, what they have *looks* like real Christianity. But it is fundamentally different, and it lacks the core of what makes a person a follower of Christ. Jesus demands that we give him our lives. It's that simple. And is that asking too much? We'd do it for a husband or wife; why not for the God of the universe?

Isn't this what baptism means for someone who comes to be baptized as an adult? The baptism is like a wedding. It is that public act by which the person says, I want to be joined to Christ—forever. I am willing to die with Jesus Christ—to go down in the grave with him, so that I might be raised with him. In faith I give all that I am, so that I may gain all that he is. And in baptism we also see visibly displayed God's pledge of commitment to us in the gospel as we are joined to Christ.

I've heard of people refusing to be baptized simply because they don't want to be seen with their hair wet! Can such a person really be a disciple of Jesus? What would you think of a bride or groom too embarrassed to get up in front of a church to say her or his wedding vows? Does that person understand what marriage is about? You'd say that such a person just doesn't get it. And many who are a part of that crowd of people who gathered around Jesus just didn't understand that when Jesus calls a man, to use the words of Dietrich Bonhoeffer, he bids him come and die. They want a casual relationship, but he won't have it. It simply can't work that way.

And what is so sad about this deception is that many people try this kind of cohabiting Christianity and find it dull, boring, and entirely unfulfilling. Consequently, they either give it up altogether or just continue to go through the motions, engaging in religious activities, with no expectations, no satisfaction, and no joy. It's the same way many people respond to a cohabiting relationship, and so they reject marriage, when, in fact, they've never tried it.

But just as God created us to prosper as men and women together in the relationship of marriage which is by definition exclusive and unconditional, so God has created us to prosper as human beings in a relationship with himself which is by definition exclusive and unconditional. Anything less is a poor imitation of the real thing.

Once we see Christ for who he is, and we taste the sweetness of his love and grace, we will not see these words of Jesus as some onerous demand upon us. Instead, we will see this as our natural response to his beauty and grace. What joy we will find in offering him more and more of ourselves! Our deepest desire will be to grow in our knowledge of Christ. This is what it means to be a disciple of Jesus Christ.

By the way, I saw a new military ad on television not long ago. It was from the marines. It said, "We don't accept applications, only commitments." I think Jesus would agree. Being a disciple of Jesus requires our all—and he desires to give you his all. There can be no greater joy than that.

NOTES

[1] Scripture quotations are from the *New International Version*, 1984.

[2] John White, *The Cost of Commitment* (Downers Grove, IL: InterVarsity Press, 1976), pp. 62-64. Used by permission of InterVarsity Press P.O. Box 1400 Downers Grove, IL 60515. www.ivpress.com.

[3] Nancy Cott, *Public Vows: A History of Marriage and the Nation* (Cambridge, MA: Harvard University Press, 2000), p. 203.

[4] That's true for all sorts of reasons, not least because that is the environment in which children are best brought into the world and nurtured into adulthood. That is the chief reason that the state has an interest in regulating, and promoting, marriage.

SCRIPTURE MEMORY VERSE

Then he called the crowd to him along with his disciples and said: "Whoever wants to be my disciple must deny themselves and take up their cross and follow me. For whoever wants to save their life will lose it, but whoever loses their life for me and for the gospel will save it. (Mark 8:35–35 NIV)

BIBLE STUDY QUESTIONS

Mark 8:31–9:1; John 15:9–11

Jesus' proclamation of the kingdom of God at the beginning of his ministry no doubt created anticipation and excitement in his disciples. But Jesus' shocking declaration that his mission leads to death on the cross turned their expectations upside down. Please read Mark 8:31–39.

1. This passage is exactly halfway through the Gospel of Mark and a couple of years into Jesus' ministry. Why do you think Jesus waited to unveil the cross?

_____

_____

_____

_____

2. The disciples went from elation to shock and denial. Are there times when you have realized that God's purposes for your life were unfolding in unexpected and even painful ways? What happened and how did you respond?

_____

_____

_____

_____

3. Having just revealed the cross, Jesus now reissues a new call for discipleship (vv. 34–38). How would you describe his discipleship challenge?

_____

_____

_____

_____

4. Jesus' call to discipleship could be rephrased, "You must die to live." How is it that, according to Jesus, following him to death makes good sense (vv. 35–37)?

_____

_____

_____

_____

5. Jesus' call to die in order to live has multiple layers of meaning; for the early church it included physical death; Cyprian (d. 258) wrote, "The blood of the martyrs was the seed of the church." What does it mean for you?

_____

_____

_____

_____

6. Jesus warned against gaining the world and losing your soul (v. 36). In what ways might the status of your soul factor into your daily decisions and motivations?

_____

_____

_____

_____

7. How might this consideration of the cost of discipleship and total surrender influence your ways of thinking, feeling, and acting?

_____

_____

_____

_____

8. In John 15:9–11, Jesus asks his disciples to obey his commands and remain in his love. What is the result of totally surrendering your all to Christ? How does that affect the way you view the cost of discipleship?

_____

_____

_____

_____

9. God is calling us to make him the highest priority in our lives, which he says will lead to joy. How can forsaking our selfish desires and following God's desire for our life lead us to greater fulfillment and joy?

_____

_____

_____

_____

10. Jesus hints in Mark 9:1 that the disciples will see the kingdom of God come with power. What power will the disciples be given to help them live out their calling to be disciples? (See Acts 1:8.) How does that power help you count the cost of discipleship?

_____

_____

_____

_____

GROUP DISCUSSION QUESTIONS

1. When Jesus calls you to be his disciple, what does he ask from you?

2. What are some of the ways in which the Scriptures and Christian writers have described Jesus' demands on your life?

3. What does Jesus offer the disciple of Christ in return for your total surrender to his will for your life?

4. How do we give Jesus total control and say in our life—to the point that we are willing to pay the cost of discipleship? When, where, and how have you given yourself to Jesus as his disciple?

5. What fears do you have that might hinder you from answering Jesus' call to give him all? (Opinions of others, risks, reputation, career, comfort, lifestyle?)

6. What does the totally committed, totally surrendered to Jesus disciple look like? What is the evidence of a live lived in obedience to Christ? Describe the traits, lifestyle, habits, and character of the person who has counted the cost.

_____

_____

7. What did Jesus mean when he said that the true disciple would "hate his father and mother, his wife and children, his brothers and sisters, yes even his own life," in order to follow Jesus?

_____

_____

8. What does Jesus mean when he asks the disciple to "carry your cross and follow me" (Mark 8:34)?

_____

_____

CHAPTER 6A

SPEAKER BIO:
WILLIAM L. "BILL" KYNES, PH.D.

SENIOR FELLOW, C.S. LEWIS INSTI-TUTE – Bill Kynes is the senior pastor of Cornerstone Evangelical Free Church, in Annandale, Virginia, where he has served since 1986. He was an undergraduate at the University of Florida with a major in philosophy. There he also played quarterback on the football team and was later inducted into the university's Athletic Hall of Fame. He attended Oxford University as a Rhodes Scholar, receiving an M.A. in theology. He received an M.Div. from Trinity Evangelical Divinity School, in Deerfield, Illinois, before returning to England for a Ph.D. in New Testament from Cambridge University.

AUTHOR BIO:
THOMAS A. TARRANTS, III, D.MIN.

VICE PRESIDENT OF MINISTRY, C.S. LEWIS INSTITUTE – Tom Tarrants has lived in the Washington D.C. area since 1978 and served as President of the C.S. Lewis Institute from 1998 to April 2010. Prior to coming to the Institute, he served as co-pastor of Christ Our Shepherd Church and Director of The School for Urban Mission, both based in Washington, D.C. He is the author of two books and is a consultant for Church Discipleship Services, developing discipleship programs and materials to strengthen the local church. Tom earned a Master of Divinity Degree from Eastern Mennonite Seminary and Doctor of Ministry from Fuller Theological Seminary.

HUMILITY AND SERVANTHOOD

When the disciples, James and John, asked Jesus if they could secure the places of prestige and honor in his kingdom, Jesus surprised them by saying, "Whoever wants to become great among you must be your servant…For even the Son of Man did not come to be served, but to serve," (Mark 10:43, 45, NIV). In God's kingdom, the virtue that is the foundation for all of the others is humility. Jesus lived this way from being born in a dirty stable, washing the disciples' feet and even laying down his life on the cross in order to save the lost. If we desire to become more like Jesus and live a fruitful life, we need to forsake pride, and embrace humility and servanthood. The purpose of this study is to lead us to a place in which we become aware of our pride, are able to commit ourselves to forsaking it, and then follow the example of Jesus by living a life of humility, serving others.

"Pride is your greatest enemy, humility is your greatest friend." So said the late John R.W. Stott, a remarkably humble man of great abilities and accomplishments; some have even said that he made the greatest impact for Christ of anyone in the twentieth century. His succinct statement about pride and humility goes straight to the heart of what the Bible teaches about the deadly root of our sins and sorrows as well as the key to God's blessing.

Pride and arrogance are conspicuous today among the rich, the powerful, the successful, celebrities of all sorts, and even some religious leaders. It is also alive and well in ordinary people, including each of us. Yet few of us realize how dangerous pride is to our souls and how much it hinders our intimacy with God and love for others. Humility, on the other hand, is often seen as weakness, and few of us know much about it or its resultant life of servanthood.

PRIDE

St. Augustine and Thomas Aquinas both taught that pride was the root of sin, as did Calvin and Luther, among others. C.S. Lewis was right when he called pride "the great sin." It is the devil's most effective and destructive tool. Why do the great spiritual leaders, Catholic, Protestant, and Eastern Orthodox, unite around this conviction? Because it is so clearly and solidly taught in Scripture.

Pride first appears in the Bible in Genesis 3, where we see the devil, that "proud spirit" as John Donne described him, using pride as the avenue by which to seduce our first parents. In just a few deft moves, he was able to use pride to bring about Eve's downfall and plunge the human race into spiritual ruin.

From this point on in the Bible, we see the outworking of pride and unbelief in the affairs of individuals, families, nations, and cultures. People lose or suppress the knowledge of God. Spiritual darkness grows, and a psychological inversion occurs; in their thinking God becomes smaller, and they become larger. The center of gravity in their mental lives shifts from God to themselves. They become the center of their world; through denial of his existence or distortion of his character, God is conveniently moved to the periphery. Self-importance and godless self-confidence grow stronger. The cycle that follows is familiar: people exalt themselves against

God and over others. Arrogant and/or abusive behavior ensues, and people suffer. On a national level, this is writ large in the history of Israel and surrounding nations, especially in the indictments delivered by the prophets of the eighth and sixth centuries BC. Blinded by power and the unprecedented affluence of the eighth century, prideful leaders in Israel embraced a corrupted view of God, trusted in their own wisdom and power, oppressed their people, ignored God's call to repent, and thereby invited his judgment, which fell with disastrous results.

There are also many biblical examples of pride and its consequences in the lives of specific individuals, and they offer valuable lessons to us. One of the more notable from the Old Testament is that of Uzziah. When he became king of Judah at age sixteen, he set his heart to seek God and put himself under the spiritual mentorship of Zechariah. And "as long as he sought the Lord, God made him to prosper" (2 Chron. 26:5).[2] As a result, he acquired wealth and became politically and militarily powerful. Then things changed. "His fame spread far, for he was marvelously helped, till he was strong. But when he was strong, he grew proud to his destruction" (26:15–16).

What happened? There are hints in the text that at some point on the road to the top, Uzziah stopped seeking the Lord and the spiritual mentoring of Zechariah. This suggests a lessening dependence on God and a growing reliance upon himself and his own strength and wisdom.

History shows at every point how easy it is for pride to increase as we become stronger, more successful, prosperous, and recognized in our endeavors. In fact, anything, real or imagined, that elevates us above others can be a platform for pride. Ironically, this is true even when these things come as a result of God's blessings. As a result of all his blessings, Uzziah, rather than humbling himself in thanksgiving to God, began to think more highly of himself than he should have and developed an exaggerated sense of his own importance and abilities. This pride of heart led to presumption before God and brought very serious consequences upon him, illustrating the biblical warnings that pride leads to disgrace (Prov. 11:2) and that "pride goes before destruction" (Prov. 16:18). I suggest that you read and meditate on the full story in 2 Chronicles. 26:1–23. The stories of Haman (Esther 3–7) and Nebuchadnezzar (Daniel 4) also offer valuable insights into pride and are well worth reading.

An instructive lesson on religious pride from the New Testament is found in the parable of the Pharisee and the tax collector (Luke 18:9–14). It is aimed at those "who trusted in themselves that they were righteous, and treated others with contempt." It addresses spiritual pride, an especially subtle and dangerous temptation of religious people and leaders. The well-known story of the Pharisee and the tax collector can help us recognize our own spiritual pride. It tells of a much-despised tax collector and a self-righteous Pharisee who go up to the temple to pray. The Pharisee proceeds to commend himself to God, because of his careful observance of the law, and look down with scornful contempt on the sinful tax collector. "God, I thank you that I am not like other men, extortioners, unjust, adulterers or even like this tax collector. I fast twice a week, I give tithes of all that I get." Notice in his prayer that his focus is not really on God at all but on how good he is and how bad others are. Here is pride wrapped in the cloak of religion and giving it a bad name. The tax collector, on the other hand, is so painfully aware of his sins and unworthiness before God that he cannot even lift his eyes as he stands in the back of the temple, far from the altar. Pounding his breast in sorrowful contrition over his sins, he can manage only the desperate plea, "God, be merciful to me, a sinner." In the Greek text, it actually reads "the sinner." His focus is very much on his own sins, not the sins of others, and especially on his need for God's mercy. In a surprising reversal of expectation, Jesus says that God answered the tax collector's prayer, not the Pharisee's. Then he concludes with his main point: "everyone who exalts himself will be humbled, but the one who humbles himself will be exalted."

It would be easy to conclude that pride is the special problem of those who are rich, powerful, successful, famous, or self-righteous. But that is wrong. It takes many shapes and forms and affects all of us to some degree.

Pride can be summarized as an attitude of self-sufficiency, self-importance, and self-exaltation in relation to God. Toward others, it is an attitude of contempt and indifference. As C.S. Lewis observed, "Pride is spiritual cancer: it eats up the very possibility of love, or contentment, or even common sense."[2] The depth of pride can vary from one person to the next and can be obvious or concealed. In the Old and New Testaments it is clear that God will not suffer the creature to exalt itself against the Creator. Pride provokes God's displeasure, and he has committed himself to oppose it. He has declared his determination to bring it low wherever he finds it, whether among angels or humans, believers or unbelievers. It was pride that caused Lucifer to be cast out of heaven and Adam and Eve to be cast out of Eden. And it is pride that will be our undoing if we tolerate it in our lives. The danger of pride is a sobering reality that each of us needs to ponder. Truly, it is our greatest enemy.

There is, of course, a good type of pride. Paul, for example, was proud of the churches he had established. But this was not arrogant or self-exalting pride. He acknowledged that his accomplishments were the fruit of God's grace to him and through him (Rom. 15:15–19). Occasionally Paul mentions boasting, but this is a matter of highlighting what God has done by his grace, either through Paul or among others. It is never self-exalting. These days most of us will say that we are proud of our children or our favorite sports team or perhaps something we have accomplished. In cases like this, we are (one hopes) saying that we are really pleased about something good and are not engaging in the sinful type of pride and arrogance the Bible condemns.

HUMILITY

Pride is a universal human problem. Everyone suffers from it to some degree. But when we have exalted ourselves in pride, God does not want to punish us and bring us low; rather, he wants to forgive and restore us. He says again and again in Scripture, humble yourselves, and I will exalt you. This gives us hope and encouragement. God takes pleasure in our efforts to humble ourselves, and he loves to bless and exalt the humble. For just as pride is the root of all sin, so "humility is the root, mother, nurse, foundation, and bond of all virtue," as John Chrysostom noted.

Admittedly, having humility and humbling of oneself is out of fashion and seems unappealing to most of us. However, as Jonathan Edwards said, "We must view humility as one of the most essential things that characterizes true Christianity." Our perspective on humility can be radically changed if we will ponder and meditate on the greatest example of humility in history, Jesus Christ. By the very act of leaving heaven, coming to earth, and taking the form of man, he demonstrated an unfathomable humbling of himself. Throughout his life on earth, Jesus, as the Suffering Servant, demonstrated a spirit of profound humility, saying that he came "not to be served, but to serve, and to give his life as a ransom for many" (Matt. 20:28). He served us in many ways, most importantly by laying down his life on the cross to purchase our salvation. So crucial was the matter of humility and service that on his last night with the disciples, Jesus took a towel and basin and washed their dirty feet, instructing them to follow his example of servanthood with one another (John 13:1–17). Andrew Murray captures it well, "Christ is the humility of God embodied in human nature; the Eternal Love humbling itself, clothing itself in the garb of meekness and gentleness, to win and serve and save us."[4]

Jesus intends servanthood to be the lifestyle of his followers. Serving others is simply the outworking of our love for him and for them. Following Jesus, the apostle Paul would later teach that "through love" we should "serve one another" (Gal. 5:13). Paul may well have been thinking of the Upper Room when he urged the believers in Philippi:

> *Have this mind among yourselves which is yours in Christ Jesus, who, though he was in the form of God, did not count equality with God a thing to be grasped, but made himself nothing, taking the form of a servant, being born in the likeness of men. And being found in human form, he humbled himself by becoming obedient to the point of death, even death on a cross. (Phil. 2:5–8)*

Here Paul is encouraging ordinary believers in a local church, who apparently have some measure of sinful pride in their hearts and relationships, to reflect on and adopt the attitude and actions of Jesus their Lord and follow his example of humble servanthood.

Those who do so will experience what Jesus experienced: exaltation by God. As Paul goes on to say, "Therefore God has highly exalted him and bestowed on him the name that is above every name, so that at the name of Jesus every knee should bow, in heaven and on earth, and under the earth and every tongue confess that Jesus Christ is Lord, to the glory of God the Father" (Phil. 2:9–11). In Jesus we have the "example of all examples": those who humble themselves will be exalted! And his example is meant to guide our earthly walk. If we will take care of humbling ourselves, we can trust God to take care of exalting us.

How do we gain the mind of Christ and humble ourselves? By making a firm decision to ponder, understand, and adopt Jesus' way of thinking; his values and attitudes must become ours. His strong emphasis on humility and meekness and his example of it must take hold of our thinking, our desires, and our conduct. We must admire his humility and want it for ourselves. This requires that we earnestly and regularly pray for the Holy Spirit to change our hearts, for it is impossible to do it in our own strength. What did Jesus mean when he called men and women to humble themselves? The Greek word that Jesus and the apostles used, *tapeinos*, conveys the idea of having a right view of ourselves before God and others.[5] If pride is an exalted sense of who we are in relation to God and others, humility is having a realistic sense of who we are before God and others. We must not think too highly (or too lowly) of ourselves. Rather, we must have an honest, sober, and realistic view of who and what we are (Rom. 12:3).

Again, Paul's advice to the Philippians is helpful, "Do nothing from rivalry or conceit, but in humility count others more significant than yourselves. Let each of you look not only to his own interests, but also to the interests of others" (Phil. 2:3–4). Refusing to be preoccupied with ourselves and our own importance and seeking to love and serve others will reorient us from self-centeredness to other-centeredness—to serving and caring for others just as Jesus did for us. In the narcissistic culture of contemporary America, this is a particularly powerful counter-cultural witness of Christ's presence and lordship in our lives.

Truly, humility is our greatest friend. It imparts the aroma of Christ to all whom we encounter. It is a sign of greatness in the kingdom of God (Luke 22:24–27). And it is the key to intimacy with God, who knows the proud from afar but dwells with him "who is of a contrite and lowly spirit (Isa. 57:15). Developing the identity, attitude, and conduct of a humble servant does not happen over night. It is rather like peeling an onion; you cut away one layer only to find another beneath it. But it does happen. As we forsake pride and seek to humble ourselves by daily deliberate choices in dependence on the Holy Spirit, humility grows in our souls. Fenelon said it well, "Humility is not a grace that can be acquired in a few months: it is the work of a lifetime." And it is a grace that is precious in the sight of God, who in due course will exalt all who embrace it.

NOTES

[1] See Augustine, *The City of God* 14.13; Thomas Aquinas, *Summa Theologica*, ques. 84.

[2] Scripture quotations are from the *English Standard Version*.

[3] C.S. Lewis, *Mere Christianity* (New York: Simon & Schuster/Touchstone, 1996), 112.

[4] Andrew Murray, *Humility* (Old Tappan, NJ: Fleming H. Revell, nd), 17.

[5] Colin Brown, *The New International Dictionary of New Testament Theology* (Grand Rapids: Zondervan, 1967), 2:259.

SCRIPTURE MEMORY VERSE

Do nothing out of selfish ambition or vain conceit, but in humility consider others better than yourselves. Each of you should look not only to your own interests, but also to the interests of others. (Philippians 2:3–4, NIV)

BIBLE STUDY QUESTIONS

Philippians 2:1–11

The founder of a movement or organization sets a tone and creates an ethos that infects all who join and shapes all that follows. It is worth pondering that Muhammad, the founder of Islam, was a general who directed armies, and Jesus, the founder of Christianity, was a teacher rejected by the Jews and crucified by the Romans. Please read Philippians 2:1–11, a passage about the qualities exhibited by Jesus.

1. There is an inner quality, a spiritual substance, that fills the soul of a mature Christian; it can infect a whole Christian community and those it touches. What words does Paul use to describe the way of life he desires for Christians (vv. 1–4)?

   Agreeing wholeheartedly with each other loving one another, working together with one purpose.

2. When and where have you seen and experienced this kind of healthy Christian community? What was it like? How did it affect you?

An outdoor church in Maui Hawaii. You could feel the love of the congregation.

3. *Self-enhancement*, *self-authenticating*, and *self-development* are popular terms used to describe the contemporary idea of psychological health. What might the apostle Paul say to such ideas (v. 3)?

Don't Be Selfish - don't live to Make a good impression on others - Be humble, thinking of others as better than yourself.

4. "Valuing others above yourself" (v. 3) may be an inspiring idea, but it is notoriously difficult to put into practice. Perhaps parents do this more than others. Why is this mode so difficult to maintain?

5. Jesus is the example and model for what Paul is advocating (v. 5). According to Paul, who is Jesus and what is it that he has done (vv. 6–11)?

Jesus was God - He did not demand
& cling to His Rights as God — He took the
humble position of a slave & appeared in
human form. He obediently humbled himself
& died died as a criminal on a cross.

6. Jesus' surrendering of his heavenly status stands in stark contrast to Adam and Eve and the rest of humanity since then (v. 6). What might happen to your emotional health and mental well-being if that which made you feel important vanished tomorrow?

PROBABLY BETTER

7. Is there a time in your life when you felt like a servant to others? What did it feel like, and how did it affect you?

Yes -

8. What changes in your attitude need to happen for you to manifest the attitude of Jesus Christ in your everyday life and relationships?

THE GREAT COMMANDMENT

LOVE OUR NEIGHBORS

9. According to Paul, the result of Jesus' humility was divine exaltation (vv. 9–11). What is his point?

Because he obeyed & became humble He was given the Name above every name every knee will bow to Jesus

10. What can you do to grow in humility? What can you do to be a servant to those around you this week?

So much – so much need

Chapter 6A – Humility and Servanthood

Group Discussion Questions

1. What are some of the ways in which the culture around us views humility?

   They view humility as weakness.

2. How did Jesus exemplify the virtue of humility in his life, death, resurrection, and ascension?

   John 11:35 Jesus wept. Jesus (God) died on the cross for our sins

3. How did the disciples respond to Jesus' words and acts of humility? How do you respond to his words and acts of humility?

   James and John wanted special seats next to Jesus in Heaven

4. How would you explain the biblical definition of humility?

   thinking of others as better than you & serving them

5. What is false humility? Give some examples.

   Golfer #1 to Golfer #2 "That was a great shot" Golfer #2 "Oh, it was nothing"

6. What are some indicators that you may be struggling with pride (i.e. critical attitude, reaction to prideful people, ways you treat people who are different)?

NEED TO TELL OTHERS OF PAST ACCOMPLISHMENTS

7. In what ways do we tend to exalt ourselves over others?

I WOULD NEVER DO WHAT SO AND SO DID

8. What is the relationship between pride and perfectionism?

WE TAKE PRIDE IN HAVING THINGS PERFECT

9. Why is it so difficult to remain humble?

WE WANT TO EXALT OURSELVES, SEPARATE
OURSELVES FROM OTHERS. "WE'RE #1"

10. What habits can we practice to help us develop the virtue of humility?

VS 14 - 15

CHAPTER 6B

SPEAKER BIO: FRANCIS ORR-EWING

DIRECTOR, LONDON FELLOWS PROGRAMME – Francis "Frog" Orr-Ewing is the Rector of Latimer Minster, oversees the Minster's weekly congregations, and has overall responsibility for the Minster projects. In 2003 he became the youngest incumbent in the country as vicar of All Saints Church in Peckham after a curacy at St. Aldates Church in Oxford. Despite Peckham's many challenges, over seven years the congregation witnessed marked growth and breakthroughs in community engagement and mission. As well as his role at the Minster, Frog is Chaplain and Missioner to the Oxford Centre for Christian Apologetics.

AUTHOR BIO: THOMAS A. TARRANTS, III, D.MIN.

VICE PRESIDENT OF MINISTRY, C.S. LEWIS INSTITUTE – Tom Tarrants has lived in the Washington D.C. area since 1978 and served as President of the C.S. Lewis Institute from 1998 to April 2010. Prior to coming to the Institute, he served as co-pastor of Christ Our Shepherd Church and Director of The School for Urban Mission, both based in Washington, D.C. He is the author of two books and is a consultant for Church Discipleship Services, developing discipleship programs and materials to strengthen the local church. Tom earned a Master of Divinity Degree from Eastern Mennonite Seminary and Doctor of Ministry from Fuller Theological Seminary.

LOVING GOD AND NEIGHBOR

God is love. Jesus lived a life of perfect love toward God and others. Jesus commands his disciples to follow his example of love and says, "'Love the Lord with all your heart and with all your soul and with all your mind.' This is the first and greatest commandment. And the second is like it: 'Love your neighbor as yourself.' All the Law and the Prophets hang on these two commandments" (Matt. 22:37–40, NIV). It is through loving God and neighbor that we are able to maximize our lives and fulfill all of the commands of God. In our culture, however, the word love *has taken on a variety of meanings, many of which don't resemble the "agape" love modeled by Christ and described in the Scriptures. If we are to become like Christ and be mature and effective disciples, we need to know what love is, and how to grow in love. The Holy Spirit will help us love if we let him lead us and he will transform us into people who love as Jesus did. For love is not a feeling, but an action. It is the intent of this study not only to give us a definition of love, but also to inspire us to love God with all of our heart, soul, mind, and strength and to love our neighbor as ourselves.*

Whether we realize it or not, we all have certain priorities in life. Some things are more important to us than others. And those that are the most important shape our lives in significant ways. This is as true for the day laborer as it is for the corporate executive. Have you ever examined your life with a view toward understanding what your priorities are? If not, you should, because for better or worse your priorities are slowly turning you into a certain kind of person and shaping your destiny.

A good way to explore our priorities is to start with what God says they should be. This will give us a framework or perspective from which to discern what our priorities really are. Fortunately, the Bible is quite clear about this. According to Jesus Christ, the first and greatest of God's commandments is to "love the Lord your God with *all* your heart and with *all* your soul and with *all* your mind" (Matt. 22:37 italics added).[1] The repetition of *all* and its application to the various aspects of our nature means that we are to love God with all that we are, with every part of our being: intellect, emotion, will, and desire. We are to become God-centered people; he is to be first in our lives, above everyone and everything, without exception. Loving God in this way is to be the first and highest priority of our lives, and from this all other priorities will find their place.

Loving God

Loving God wholeheartedly lies at the heart of spiritual health, and the more we love him the healthier we are. Echoing the spiritual giants throughout history, C.S. Lewis says, "Every Christian would agree that a man's spiritual health is exactly proportional to his love for God."[2] Do you agree? Is wholehearted love for God the highest priority in *your* life?

To rightly answer this question, we must begin with a basic understanding of what the Bible means by the word *God*. This is necessary because our view of God has such profound personal implications. As A.W. Tozer said, "What comes into our minds when we think about God is the most important thing about us."[3] Discerning the biblical view of God is also important because many Americans who say they believe in God use the word to mean something other than the God of the Bible. And even those who do mean the God of the Bible sometimes have distorted ideas and images of him that hinder their ability to love him wholeheartedly.

In the Bible, the word *God* describes an invisible and eternal spiritual being who is immense and infinitely powerful, wise, knowing, and good. He is holy, morally pure, loving, gracious, merciful, patient, and forgiving. He created and sustains all things, seen and unseen, and will one day judge all mankind. Much more could be said, but this brief description helps us distinguish the God of the Bible from other gods. Is this what comes into your mind when you think about God? This is the God whom Jesus says we are to love wholeheartedly.

How do we love this God? We must first come to know him, for it is impossible to love someone you do not know. Coming to know God involves gaining true and accurate knowledge about him. Although he has shown us something of his eternal power and divine nature in creation (Rom. 1:20), it is preeminently in the Scriptures that he has given us true, accurate, and detailed knowledge about himself and his ways. This propositional knowledge *about* God is a necessary and indispensable foundation for knowing him, but is not sufficient by itself. With the help of the Holy Spirit, we must go on to *meet God personally* and know him in a relational way. This happens as we come to believe what we have learned about him and entrust ourselves to him. God has given the clearest revelation of himself to us in Jesus, who said, "Whoever has seen me has seen the Father" (John 14:9), and whom Paul described as "the image of the invisible God" (Col. 1:15). Jesus calls us to "repent and believe the gospel" (Mark 1:15). And as we respond to his call with faith in him and his atoning sacrifice on the cross, we come to know God and Christ in a saving and relational way.

Once we come to know God, we experience a fundamental inner change that enables and inspires us to love God. This change is produced by the Holy Spirit, who comes to dwell within us and produces a new life (John 3:5–8), and a love for God and others (Rom. 5:5). Whereas we were once dead to God, we are now alive to him. Whereas we were formerly his enemy, now we are his friend and love him. This radical change gives us a new outlook on life along with new desires and power to live a new life.

However, this spiritual "new birth" is just the beginning. After our conversion, we are in a state of infancy and need proper care and feeding in order to grow in our new relationship with God. The spiritual nurture that helps us mature comes to us, as it did to the first believers, in a community *devoted* to four things: "to the apostles' teaching and the fellowship, to the breaking of bread and the prayers" (Acts 2:42). The combination of these four elements creates a sort of "spiritual incubator" for growing in the knowledge and love of God and of Jesus. Belonging to such a community is vital and *devoting* ourselves to all four means of grace is essential for growing to maturity. Each one is necessary, and none can be neglected without significant loss.

But being in the incubator doesn't guarantee that we will grow in love for God. A vital but often overlooked aspect of our spiritual growth is how we respond to what we learn about God, especially in Scripture. As we *devote* ourselves to reading, studying, memorizing, and meditating on what the Bible teaches about God's nature, character, and will we become aware of things in our lives that need to change. This confronts us with an unavoidable decision: will we obey or disobey his Word? Will we change or refuse to change? If we disobey, our disobedience interrupts our fellowship with God and can stall or even seriously derail our spiritual growth (until we repent and obey). Some people have made a shipwreck of their lives by refusing to obey God's Word.

But if we obey God, we will grow stronger, and our knowledge and love for him will increase. Loving obedience is the key. As the apostle John said, "This is the love of God, that we keep his commandments. And his commandments are not burdensome" (1 John 5:3). God's commands are an expression of holy love and are given for our good and his glory. They are the instructions of a loving father to his little children. And our obedience expresses our grateful love and brings him pleasure. Jesus, who was God in human form, makes it crystal clear: "If you love me, you will keep my commandments" (John 14:15), and "Whoever has my commandments and keeps them, he it is who loves me. And he who loves me will be loved by my Father, and I will love him and manifest (i.e., show or disclose) myself to him" (John 14:21). Obedience is the fruit of grace and love and has as its reward a deeper experiential knowledge of Christ. As John Stott puts it, "The test of love is obedience and the reward of love is the self-manifestation of Christ."[4]

LOVING OUR NEIGHBOR

To the first and greatest commandment, Jesus added a second, which is inseparable from it: "You shall love your neighbor as yourself" (Matt. 22:39). It takes but little reflection to realize that like the first, this is a very challenging command. People have often commented that loving God is a lot easier than loving one's neighbor. And most of us know at least one person who proves the truth of this observation. But that does not excuse us from loving our neighbor, for obedience to this command is a concrete manifestation of our love for God.

What does it mean to love our neighbor? Again we need to clarify our terms, this time, *love*. Because it is often used in contemporary English to denote feeling and sentiment, we can easily assume that to "love" our neighbor is to have warm and positive feelings toward him or her.

However, this is an error that can hinder us from loving our neighbor. The fact is that we do not have such feelings toward all people and cannot manufacture them. If loving our neighbor required this, we would be in a hopelessly impossible situation and tempted to give up our faith.

The good news is that our English word *love* is used to translate the Greek word *agape*. And *agape* is not a word that denotes feeling or sentiment. Rather, it focuses on the will. Thus the fundamental nature of the command to love our neighbor is a matter of will, not feeling. Jesus was a realist, and he knew that we cannot command our feelings to be warm when they are cold or positive when they are negative. But we can exercise our will to act in another person's best interest no matter how we happen to feel about that person.

This understanding underlies Jesus' simple and practical instructions for loving others: "Whatever you wish that others would do to you, do also to them, for this is the Law and the Prophets" (Matt. 7:12). Have you ever wondered how to love someone as God commands? This is your answer. Consider the circumstances of the person before you and treat that person the way you would want to be treated if you were in his shoes. To act in that person's best interests, regardless of what you feel or don't feel, is to love as Jesus intends.

This can be easy or hard. It may not be a great challenge to love a friend or family member if the sacrifice is not great. But loving one's neighbor cannot be limited to what is easy or convenient. In the story of the Good Samaritan, Jesus made it clear that a neighbor is anyone in our path who needs our help, whether helping is easy or not, convenient or not (Luke 10:29–37). Indeed, rendering such help can be dangerous and financially costly, as well (10:34–35).

When our neighbor is a fellow disciple in the family of God, the standard rises to a higher level. On the night he was betrayed, Jesus said to his followers, "A new commandment I give to you, that you love one another: just as I have loved you, you also are to love one another. By this all people will know that you are my disciples, if you have love for one another" (John 13:34–35). He went on to clarify the implications of this love when he said, "Greater love has no one than this, that someone lays down his life for his friends" (John 15:13). Far from an abstract concept or a momentary sentiment, this moves us to a concrete, practical love. This kind of love shaped the understanding and practice of his disciples and the early church, of which we are told, "There was not a needy person among them, for as many as were owners of lands or houses sold them ... and it was distributed to each as any had need" (Acts 4:34–35). And decades later we find the apostle John saying, "By this we know love, that he laid down his life for us, and we ought to lay down our lives for the brothers. But if anyone has the world's goods and sees his brother in need, yet closes his heart against him, how does God's love abide in him?

Little children, let us not love in word or talk but in deed and in truth" (1 John 3:16–18). At a minimum, this means that we are to be alert to the material needs of our brothers and sisters and to show our love by helping them financially as we are able.

When our neighbor is an enemy, we face perhaps the most difficult test of love. Jesus boldly calls his followers to love their enemies:

> *I say to you, Love your enemies and pray for those who persecute you, so that you may be sons of your Father who is in heaven. For he makes his sun to rise on the evil and on the good, and sends rain on the just and on the unjust. For if you love those who love you, what reward do you have? Do not even the tax collectors do the same? And if you greet only your brothers, what more are you doing than others? Do not even the Gentiles do the same? You therefore must be perfect, as your heavenly Father is perfect." (Matt. 5:44–47)*

In this passage, Jesus calls us to pursue a perfect (i.e., mature) love, to love in the way our heavenly Father loves.

For many of us, this command is profoundly disturbing. In fact, the more clearly we understand what it really means to love God and neighbor, the more we realize just how impossible it is, at least in our own strength. At this point, we may be tempted to see it as impossible idealism. But it is not impossible idealism. Jesus is serious; he intends us to pursue love as our first priority in life and to become filled with love. And it is possible to love as he commands—not with absolute perfection, but certainly with increasing maturity and fullness. Astonishing growth is possible if we will seek it.

How do we seek it? Clearly, love for God is not something of our own making, for we are by nature God's enemies (Rom. 8:7). If loving God and others were dependent on us, it would be hopeless, impossible idealism. But once we believe the gospel and trust Christ, the Holy Spirit comes to dwell in us, bringing new life (John 3:6) and pouring God's love into our hearts (Rom. 5:5). This evokes and enables our love for God. As John says, "In this is love, not that we loved God but that he loved us and sent his Son to be the propitiation for our sins" (1 John 4:10). Our love for God is an answering love, a love that is awakened by his prior love for us, made real to us by the Spirit. Assurance of God's fatherly love for us is the root of our love for him. And the more we meditate on and embrace his love for us, especially at the cross, the more our love for him and others grows.

The Holy Spirit is the ultimate source of love in our lives and is charged with making us into people of love. For this love to grow, we must daily seek to be filled with the Holy Spirit (Eph. 5:18) and to walk in the Spirit (Gal. 5:16). And likewise we must seek to avoid grieving or

quenching the Spirit in what we think, desire, say, and do. As we live in the Spirit, he will produce deep and powerful changes within us: "love, joy, peace, patience, kindness, goodness, faithfulness, gentleness, self-control" (Gal. 5:22). These changes begin when the Spirit enters our lives, and we mature over time, growing faster or slower depending on whether we are in a healthy spiritual environment and how we respond to God. As mentioned earlier, we need to be in a community *devoted* to Scripture, fellowship, worship, and prayer. We also need a hunger for God and a wholehearted commitment to him (Rom. 12:1–2); we must respond to him in faith and obedience. These are essential for healthy spiritual growth and maturing love.

One final point. Even when we are making our best effort to live in the Spirit and to love God and others, we are not immune to sin. We are always faced with the choice of yielding to the Spirit or to the flesh. Whether it is a long-standing, deeply ingrained pattern of sin or a flaw in temperament or something else, we are vulnerable to temptation. And sometimes we yield to the flesh and commit sin. When we do, we can be restored through repentance, confession, and returning to the Lord. He is "good and forgiving, abounding in steadfast love to all who call upon [him]" (Ps. 86:5).

This brings us back to where we started. "Whether we realize it or not, we all have certain priorities in life. Some things are more important to us than others. And those that are the most important shape our lives in significant ways ... For better or worse your priorities are slowly turning you into a certain kind of person and shaping your destiny." Jesus says that loving God wholeheartedly and loving our neighbor as ourselves are the two highest priorities of life. If you will make these the highest priorities in your life and pursue them with the Spirit's help, you will be steadily transformed into a person of love who glorifies God and experiences the greatest fulfillment possible in this life. The choice is yours.

NOTES

[1] Scripture quotations are from the *English Standard Version*.

[2] C.S. Lewis, *The Four Loves* (1960; repr., New York: Harcourt/Harvest, 1991), 3.

[3] A.W. Tozer, *The Knowledge of the Holy* (New York: HarperCollins, 1961), 1.

[4] John R.W. Stott, *Christ the Liberator* (Downers Grove, IL: InterVarsity Press, 1971), 39.

Scripture Memory Verse

"Teacher, which is the greatest commandment in the Law?" Jesus replied: "'Love the Lord your God with all your heart and with all your soul and with all your mind.' This is the first and greatest commandment. And the second is like it: 'Love your neighbor as yourself.' All the Law and the Prophets hang on these two commandments." (Matthew 22:36–40, NIV)

Bible Study Questions

Matthew 22:34–40; Luke 10:25–37

What do Oxford University, the Red Cross, and Harvard Medical School have in common? They were all founded as Christian institutions. Since Jesus established the church, it has been the source of education, social care, and medical skill around the world and through the ages. At the heart of the Christian life is a powerful motivation to care for others as well as encourage public and private morally responsible behavior.

Let's look at two scriptural passages that take us to the heart of these social and spiritual riches. Please read Matthew 22:34–40.

1. The poets and song writers of the world are right: love really is the most important thing in the world. Compare and contrast Jesus' teaching on love with your sense of the poets' and musicians' message on love.

_____

_____

_____

_____

2. Jesus' teaching on the love of God is comprehensive, mental, and passionate, that is, it encompasses the heart, soul, and mind (v. 37). Who comes to mind when you think about people who love God? How have those people affected you?

_____

_____

_____

_____

3. How does the love of God shape your life, both your thoughts and actions?

_____

_____

_____

_____

4. Jesus says that the Law and the Prophets, that is, the Old Testament, "hangs" on loving God and neighbor (v. 39). How does this square with your understanding of the spirit and central theme of the Old Testament?

_____

_____

_____

_____

5. Loving God precedes loving your neighbor. What happens if the order is reversed, or if the love of God is left out?

_____

_____

_____

_____

6. How does Jesus' parable of the Good Samaritan, in Luke 10:25–37, illustrate his teaching on love?

_____

_____

_____

_____

7. How can social prejudice inhibit our practice of love and its expressions of compassion toward others?

_____

_____

_____

_____

8. Jesus is inextricably tying together morality, social responsibility, and devotion to God. How are these three woven together in your life?

_____

_____

_____

_____

9. Jesus addresses our motivation. What is the difference between moral behavior and social compassion motivated by love and that motivated by duty?

_____

_____

_____

_____

10. As in this parable, love throughout the Bible is not primarily an emotion but a motivation and action. How might this make a difference in the way you love God and others?

_____

_____

_____

_____

GROUP DISCUSSION QUESTIONS

1. What are some of the different definitions of love that you have encountered in your lifetime?

_____

_____

2. How is the biblical definition of love different from the other definitions of love prevalent in society?

_____

_____

3. If love isn't a feeling, how can we know that we are actually being loving?

_____

_____

4. Why should we obey God's word and his moral commands?

_____

_____

5. What are some examples of God's love for us?

_____

_____

6. What are some ways in which we can show our love for God? For our neighbor?

    _____

    _____

7. What steps can we take in our society, family, and church to become more loving toward God and neighbor?

    _____

    _____

8. The Bible often mentions taking care of the orphans and widows—the poor, as a way of loving our neighbor. How well are we doing at demonstrating God's love for the least of these in our personal lives, family, and church?

    _____

    _____

9. What disciplines or habits can we practice to help us grow in the area of loving God and neighbor?

    _____

    _____

CHAPTER 7

SPEAKER BIO: ARTHUR W. LINDSLEY, PH.D.

SENIOR FELLOW, C.S. LEWIS INSTITUTE – Art Lindsley has served at the C.S. Lewis Institute since 1987. Formerly, he was Director of Educational Ministries at the Ligonier Valley Study Center, and Staff Specialist with the Coalition for Christian Outreach. He is the author of *C.S. Lewis's Case for Christ, True Truth, Love: The Ultimate Apologetic*, and co-author with R.C. Sproul and John Gerstner of *Classical Apologetics*, and has written numerous articles on theology, apologetics, C.S. Lewis, and the lives and works of many other authors and teachers. Art earned his M.Div. from Pittsburgh Theological Seminary and a Ph.D. in Religious Studies from the University of Pittsburgh. He is currently the Vice President of Theological Initiatives for the Institute for Faith, Work and Economics.

AUTHOR BIO: KENNETH BOA, PH.D.

PRESIDENT, REFLECTIONS MINISTRIES – Ken Boa is the President of Reflections Ministries, an organization that seeks to encourage, teach, and equip people to know Christ. He is also President of Trinity House Publishers. Some of Dr. Boa's recent publications include: *Conformed to His Image, 20 Compelling Evidences that God Exists*, and *Augustine to Freud*. He holds a Bachelor of Science degree from Case Institute of Technology, a Master of Theology degree from Dallas Theological Seminary, a Doctorate from New York University, and a Doctor of Philosophy degree from the University of Oxford in England.

AUTHORITY OF THE BIBLE

Jesus quoted the Scriptures of his day, what we now call the Old Testament, as if they were the true, inspired, and authoritative Word of God. And until the past couple of centuries, most people in the West accepted the authority of the Bible over life and faith. However, in recent times, the Bible has come under attack from both outside and inside the church. This question of the authority of the Bible plays a key role in shaping the way in which we live our lives as disciples of Jesus. If the Bible is just like any other piece of literature with a few good lines, it has no authority over us and is of little importance. On the other hand, if it really is God's revealed word to us, and we are expected to obey its teaching, the conclusion must be that the Bible is of the utmost importance. We must take it seriously and it should impact every area of life. For that reason, this study hopes to give you a hunger for more of God's Word as it is found in the inspired, authoritative Bible.

"You're always quoting the Bible to me as if it were the last word on issues about life. How can you base your life on a book that's so full of contradictions and errors? Historians and scientists have long since proven that the Bible is inaccurate and unreliable."

Many people are of the opinion that the teachings of the Bible are outdated, contradictory, and full of scientific and historical errors. With few exceptions, they have reached these conclusions through second- and third-hand sources rather than their own study of the Bible. Consider the following statements:

- The Bible says that God helps those who help themselves.
- The books of the New Testament were written centuries after the events they describe.
- "Cleanliness is next to godliness" is in the Bible.
- According to the Bible, the earth is flat.
- The earliest New Testament manuscripts go back only to the fourth or fifth centuries A.D.
- The Bible teaches that the earth is the center of the universe.
- The English Bible is a translation of a translation of a translation (etc.) of the original, and fresh errors were introduced in each stage of the process.

How many of these statements do you think are true? The answer is that all of them are false. Yet these false impressions persist in the minds of many, and misinformation like this produces a skeptical attitude toward the Bible.

In this article, we will consider a number of objections to the accuracy and reliability of the Bible to help you make a more informed decision as to whether or not it is authoritative.

"How can you be sure that the Bible is the same now as when it was written? The Bible has been copied and translated so many times! Haven't you ever played the game where people sit in circle and pass a sentence from one person to the next until it comes back around in a completely distorted version? If that could happen in a room in just a few minutes, think of all the errors and changes that must have filled the Bible in the centuries since it was first written!"

There are three lines of evidence that support the claim that the biblical documents are reliable: the bibliographic test, the internal test, and the external test. The first test examines the biblical manuscripts, the second deals with the claims made by the biblical authors, and the third looks to outside confirmation of the biblical content.

THE BIBLIOGRAPHIC TEST

The Quantity of Manuscripts

In the case of the Old Testament, there are a small number of Hebrew manuscripts, because Jewish scribes ceremonially buried imperfect and worn manuscripts. Many ancient manuscripts were lost or destroyed during Israel's turbulent history. Also, the Old Testament text was standardized by the Masoretic Jews by the sixth century A.D., and all manuscripts that deviated from the Masoretic Text were eliminated. But the existing Hebrew manuscripts are supplemented by the Dead Sea Scrolls, the Septuagint (a third-century B.C. Greek translation of the Old Testament), the Samaritan Pentateuch, and the Targums (ancient paraphrases of the Old Testament), as well as the Talmud (teachings and commentaries related to the Hebrew Scriptures).

The quantity of New Testament manuscripts is unparalleled in ancient literature. There are over five thousand Greek manuscripts, eight thousand Latin manuscripts, and another thousand manuscripts in other languages (Syriac, Coptic, etc.). In addition to this extraordinary number, there are tens of thousands of citations of New Testament passages by the early church fathers. In contrast, the typical number of existing manuscript copies for any of the works of the Greek and Latin authors, such as Plato, Aristotle, Caesar, or Tacitus, ranges from one to twenty.

The Quality of Manuscripts

Because of the great reverence the Jewish scribes held toward the Scriptures, they exercised extreme care in making new copies of the Hebrew Bible. The entire scribal process was specified in meticulous detail to minimize the possibility of even the slightest error. The letters, words, and lines were counted, and the middle letters of the Pentateuch and the Old Testament were determined. If a single mistake was discovered, the entire manuscript was destroyed.

As a result of this extreme care, the quality of the manuscripts of the Hebrew Bible surpasses all other ancient manuscripts. The 1947 discovery of the Dead Sea Scrolls provided a significant check, because these Hebrew scrolls antedate the earliest Masoretic Old Testament manuscripts by about a thousand years. But in spite of this time span, the number of variant readings between the Dead Sea Scrolls and the Masoretic Text is quite small, and most of these are variations in spelling and style.

While the quality of the Old Testament manuscripts is excellent, that of the New Testament is very good—considerably better than the manuscript quality of other ancient documents. Because of the thousands of New Testament manuscripts, there are many variant readings, but these variants are actually used by scholars to reconstruct the original readings by determining which variant best explains the others in any given passage. Some of these variant readings crept into the manuscripts because of visual errors in copying or because of auditory errors when a group of scribes copied manuscripts that were read aloud. Other errors resulted from faulty writing, memory, and judgment, and still others from well-meaning scribes who thought they were correcting the text. Nevertheless, only a small number of these differences affect the sense of the passages, and only a fraction of these have any real consequences. Furthermore, no variant readings are significant enough to call into question any of the doctrines of the New Testament. The New Testament can be regarded as 99.5 percent pure, and the correct readings for the remaining 0.5 percent can often be ascertained with a fair degree of probability by the practice of textual criticism.

The Time Span of Manuscripts

Apart from some fragments, the earliest Masoretic manuscript of the Old Testament is dated at A.D. 895, due to the systematic destruction of worn manuscripts by the Masoretic scribes. However, the discovery of the Dead Sea Scrolls dating from 200 B.C. to A.D. 68 drastically reduced the time span from the writing of the Old Testament books to our earliest copies of them.

The time span of the New Testament manuscripts is exceptional. The manuscripts on papyrus came from the second and third centuries A.D. The John Rylands Fragment (P52) of the Gospel of John is dated at A.D. 117–138, only a few decades after the Gospel was written. The Bodmer Papyri are dated from A.D. 175–225, and the Chester Beatty Papyri date from about A.D. 250. The time span for most of the New Testament is less than two hundred years (and some are within one hundred years) from the date of authorship to the date of our earliest manuscripts. This sharply contrasts with the average gap of more than one thousand between the composition and the earliest copy of the writings of other ancient authors.

To summarize the bibliographic test, the Old and New Testaments enjoy far greater manuscript attestation in terms of quantity, quality, and time span than any other ancient documents. It is especially interesting to make specific comparisons between the New Testament and other writings.

THE INTERNAL TEST

The second test of the reliability of the biblical documents asks, "What claims does the Bible make about itself?" This may appear to be circular reasoning. It sounds like we are using the testimony of the Bible to prove that the Bible is true. But we are really examining the truth claims of the various authors of the Bible and allowing them to speak for themselves. (Remember that the Bible is not one book but many books woven together.) This provides significant evidence that must not be ignored.

A number of biblical authors claim that their accounts are primary, not secondary. That is, the bulk of the Bible was written by people who were eyewitnesses of the events they recorded. John wrote in his gospel, "And he who has seen has borne witness, and his witness is true; and he knows that he is telling the truth, so that you also may believe" (John 19:35; see 21:24).[1] In his first epistle, John wrote, "What was from the beginning, what we have heard, what we have seen with our eyes, what we beheld and our hands handled concerning the Word of life ... what we have seen and heard we proclaim to you also" (1 John 1:1, 3). Peter makes the same point abundantly clear: "For we did not follow cleverly devised tales when we made known to you the power and coming of our Lord Jesus Christ, but we were eyewitnesses of His majesty" (2 Pet. 1:16; also see Acts 2:22; 1 Pet. 5:1).

The independent eyewitness accounts in the New Testament of the life, death, and resurrection of Christ were written by people who were intimately acquainted with Jesus Christ. Their gospels and epistles reveal their integrity and complete commitment to the truth, and they maintained their testimony even through persecution and martyrdom. All the evidence inside and outside the New Testament runs contrary to the claim made by form criticism that the early church distorted the life and teachings of Christ. Most of the New Testament was written between A.D. 47 and 70, and all of it was complete before the end of the first century. There simply was not enough time for myths about Christ to be created and propagated. And the multitudes of eyewitnesses who were alive when the New Testament books began to be circulated would have challenged blatant historical fabrications about the life of Christ. The Bible places great stress on accurate historical details, and this is especially obvious in the Gospel of Luke and the book of Acts, Luke's two-part masterpiece (see his prologue in Luke 1:1–4).

CHAPTER 7 – AUTHORITY OF THE BIBLE

THE EXTERNAL TEST

Because the Scriptures continually refer to historical events, they are verifiable; their accuracy can be checked by external evidence. The chronological details in the prologue to Jeremiah (1:1–3) and in Luke 3:1–2 illustrate this. Ezekiel 1:2 allows us to date Ezekiel's first vision of God to the day (July 31, 592 B.C.).

The historicity of Jesus Christ is well-established by early Roman, Greek, and Jewish sources, and these extrabiblical writings affirm the major details of the New Testament portrait of the Lord. The first-century Jewish historian Flavius Josephus made specific references to John the Baptist, Jesus Christ, and James in his *Antiquities of the Jews*. In this work, Josephus gives us many background details about the Herods, the Sadducees and Pharisees, the high priests like Annas and Caiaphas, and the Roman emperors mentioned in the Gospels and Acts.

We find another early secular reference to Jesus in a letter written a little after A.D. 73 by an imprisoned Syrian named Mara Bar-Serapion. This letter to his son compares the deaths of Socrates, Pythagoras, and Christ. Other first- and second-century writers who mention Christ include the Roman historians Cornelius Tacitus (*Annals*) and Suetonius (*Life of Claudius, Lives of the Caesars*), the Roman governor Pliny the Younger (*Epistles*), and the Greek satirist Lucian (*On the Death of Peregrine*). Jesus is also mentioned a number of times in the Jewish Talmud.

The Old and New Testaments make abundant references to nations, kings, battles, cities, mountains, rivers, buildings, treaties, customs, economics, politics, dates, etc. Because the historical narratives of the Bible are so specific, many of its details are open to archaeological investigation. While we cannot say that archaeology proves the authority of the Bible, it is fair to say that archaeological evidence has provided external confirmation of hundreds of biblical statements. Higher criticism in the nineteenth century made many damaging claims that would completely overthrow the integrity of the Bible, but the explosion of archaeological knowledge in the twentieth century reversed almost all of these claims. Noted archaeologists such as William F. Albright, Nelson Glueck, and G. Ernest Wright developed a great respect for the historical accuracy of the Scriptures as a result of their work.

Out of the multitude of archaeological discoveries related to the Bible, consider a few examples to illustrate the remarkable external substantiation of biblical claims. Excavations at Nuzi (1925–1941), Mari (discovered in 1933), and Alalakh (1937–1939; 1946–1949) provide helpful background information that fits well with the Genesis stories of the patriarchal period. The Nuzi tablets and Mari letters illustrate the patriarchal customs in great detail, and the Ras Shamra tablets discovered in ancient Ugarit in Syria shed much light on Hebrew prose and poetry and Canaanite culture. The Ebla tablets discovered recently in northern Syria also affirm the antiquity and accuracy of the book of Genesis.

Some scholars once claimed that the Mosaic Law could not have been written by Moses, because writing was largely unknown at that time and because the law code of the Pentateuch was too sophisticated for that period. But the codified Laws of Hammurabi (ca. 1700 B.C.), the Lipit-Ishtar code (ca. 1860 B.C.), the Laws of Eshnunna (ca. 1950 B.C.), and the even earlier Ur-Nammu code have refuted these claims.

Much more could be said about the reliability of the Bible. Hopefully, this article gives you a sense of some of the responses which can be made to the questions of skeptics. For more, consult some of the many excellent books on this topic.

NOTES

[1]Scripture quotations are from the *New American Standard Bible*.

SCRIPTURE MEMORY VERSE

All Scripture is God-breathed and is useful for teaching, rebuking, correcting and training in righteousness, so that the man of God may be thoroughly equipped for every good work. (2 Timothy 3:16–17, NIV)

BIBLE STUDY QUESTIONS

2 Timothy 3:15–17 and 2:15

Our understanding of the value and importance of the Bible can be enhanced as we listen in on Paul's letter to Timothy about the usefulness of the Holy Scriptures. Please read 2 Timothy 3:15–17.

1. The word *holy* means unique, special, distinct, and close to God. From your own experience, how is it that the Bible is different from other books or writings that address God and spiritual issues?

_____

_____

_____

_____

2. Paul tells Timothy to pay attention to the Holy Scriptures because they bring a special kind of wisdom. What does it mean to be *wise* as the word is used in 3:15?

_____

_____

_____

_____

3. The primary classic purpose of education, going all the way back to the Greeks, was to teach children what they should love and what they should hate. How have the Scriptures been helpful in educating you?

_____

_____

_____

_____

4. We should pay attention to the Scriptures for another reason: because they are "God-breathed"—inspired by God (v. 16). Why is it important for you personally to keep in mind that Scriptures are inspired rather than merely inspiring?

_____

_____

_____

_____

5. Inspiration brings authority. There is a moral obligation to believe and obey what God says. How does "teaching," "rebuking," and "correcting" (v. 16) connect us to the moral authority of the Scriptures?

_____

_____

_____

_____

6. Of course the Scriptures are indeed inspiring as well as inspired. How are you inspired by them?

_____

_____

_____

_____

7. Paul gives a third reason to pay attention to the Scriptures: they are useful "for equipping for every good work" (v. 17). For what good works would you like to be equipped, and how might the Scriptures help you?

_____

_____

_____

_____

8. In the previous chapter, Paul admonishes Timothy to be "a workman ... who correctly handles the word of truth" (2:15). What does the idea of workman add to the way you could think about approaching the Holy Scriptures?

9. In learning to "handle the Scriptures," what have you found pleasurable? Difficult?

10. A good workman is a good craftsman. How would you like to grow as a craftsman of the Scriptures?

GROUP DISCUSSION QUESTIONS

1. What views did you have of Scripture when you were growing up? As you got older?

2. What are some other views of the Bible's authority that you have encountered? How have you seen the Bible come under attack?

3. What are some of the reasons why we can adhere to the reliability and the trustworthiness of the Bible? Elaborate.

4. What are some dangers we can encounter if we pick and choose what parts of the Bible we want to practice and believe and disregard or discredit the other parts?

5. If we believe that the Bible is God's Word, what implications does that have in the way in which we live our lives in society, the church, and the family?

_____

_____

6. What particular areas of the Bible do you find most difficult to believe or obey?

_____

_____

7. What practices can help you gain a deeper understanding of God's Word and help you in obeying God's Word? How has the Bible helped you throughout your life? Give some examples.

_____

_____

CHAPTER 8

SPEAKER BIO:
AMY ORR-EWING

TRAINING DIRECTOR, RZIM ZACH-ARIAS TRUST – Amy oversees the Trust's apologetics training programme, and lectures not only at the Oxford Centre for Christian Apologetics but also at many universities, churches and conferences. She is coauthor with her husband, Francis "Frog" Orr-Ewing, of *Holy Warriors: A Fresh Look at the Face of Extreme Islam* and has contributed to the book *God and the Generations*. Her new book *Why Trust the Bible?* (published under the title *Is the Bible Intolerant?* in North America) was shortlisted for the 2006 UK Christian Book Awards. Amy holds a degree in theology from Christ Church, Oxford University, and a Masters degree in Theology from King's College, London.

AUTHOR BIO:
BILL SMITH, M.DIV

DIRECTOR, C.S. LEWIS INSTITUTE - ATLANTA – Bill Smith is the president and founder of On the Way Ministries, an equipping ministry devoted to renewing the mind, engaging the heart, and encouraging community. He teaches in a variety of contexts including churches, schools, businesses, conference/retreat centers, coffeehouses, bookstores, and homes. He is the author of *Conversations on the Question of God with C.S. Lewis and Sigmund Freud*, a companion guide to the PBS DVD series *The Question of God*. He holds a B.S. in Biblical Studies from Toccoa Falls College and a M.Div. from Trinity Evangelical Divinity School.

THE PRACTICE OF PRAYER

Prayer for the disciple of Christ is like breathing. It is essential for maintaining a vibrant and healthy spiritual life. Any good relationship needs regular and honest communication. Prayer is one of the primary ways in which we build our relationship with our heavenly Father. A simple definition of prayer is "talking with God." That implies a two-way conversation in which we are both listening to him and sharing our thoughts with him. And the good news is that the Lord desires to be in a communicative relationship with us. The bad news is that our own sinful nature, the pressures of life in this world, and the evil one conspire daily to hinder our prayer life. The intent of this study is to both encourage us to enjoy the gift of prayer daily and to battle all the forces that would try to prevent us from growing in our relationship with the Lord.

> If prayer is talking to God, who is this God we talk to? At the level of our human experience, we can assert the following: how we talk to people, and what we say, will to a large extent be governed by how well we know them.
>
> —Graeme Goldsworthy, *Prayer and the Knowledge of God*[1]

Prayer has been defined very concisely as "personal communication with God."[2] While most people say that they believe in prayer, many have never given much thought to how their practice of prayer relates to their beliefs about the One to whom they pray. Since prayer is about communication with God, it only makes sense that how we pray, what we expect from prayer, and what we experience in prayer are directly related to our understanding of who God is, who we are as human beings, and what kind of world we live in. Jesus taught about prayer on a number of occasions but our focus will be on what is commonly referred to as the Lord's Prayer (Matt. 6:9–13).

Jesus purposefully begins by focusing our attention on the character of the One whom we address in prayer. He says that we are to pray to *"Our Father in heaven."*[3] In the Old Testament, God is referred to as a Father in relationship to his people (Deut.; 32:6), and Israel is called God's son in several places (Exod. 4:22; Hos. 11:1), but it is most significant that the fatherhood of God is directly connected to the relationship between God and Israel's promised Messiah (Ps. 89:27–28). Matthew emphasizes that Jesus is the long-awaited Messiah, the son of David (Matt. 1:1; 16:16) who comes to "save his people" (Matt. 1:21) and usher in God's rule.

It was virtually unheard of to address God as Father in Jesus' day. Our privilege of knowing and communicating with God as Father is based on our union with Jesus the Son. Through being united to the Son, we experience new birth (John 1:12) and are encouraged by the Holy Spirit to call out to God as Father (Gal. 4:4–7). Andrew Murray says:

The knowledge of God's Father-love is the first and simplest but also the last and highest lesson in the school of prayer. Prayer begins in the personal relationship with the living God as well as the personal, conscious fellowship of love with Him. In the knowledge of God's Fatherness revealed by the Holy Spirit, the power of prayer will root and grow. The life of prayer has its joy in the infinite tenderness, care, and patience of an infinite Father who is ready to hear and to help.

—Andrew Murray, *With Christ in the School of Prayer*[A]

The fatherhood of God is revealed most clearly through the words and actions of his Son, Jesus the Messiah (John 14:7–9). The apostle Paul tells us that the Spirit of the Son moves us to pray to God as Abba-Father (Gal. 4:6). Having grounded prayer in the context of familial relationship, Jesus in Matthew 6 moves on to teach us about the God-centered motives that should shape our requests.

We should pray, *"Hallowed be your name."* The word *hallowed* is the verbal form of the word *holy,* which means to set apart. God is *holy* because he is unique. The prayer that God's name be made holy is not a request that God would become something that he is not, but that we might recognize him for who he is. The prayer for God's name to be hallowed is a prayer for people to become aware of the greatness and goodness of God. Too often spirituality is just another tool for realizing our self-potential, but Jesus reminds us that our lives are most in line with reality when we develop a God-centeredness that places his glory at the center of reality.

We can see the same kind of adjustment of priorities in the prayer *"Your kingdom come, your will be done on earth as it is in heaven."* Jesus knew that our ultimate hope must lie in the coming of God's kingdom, his rule. It is only through God's liberating presence (word and spirit) that the effects of sin and corruption are overcome. Though we know that the full realization of God's promises will not come until Jesus returns, we pray in faith and persevere in hope, asking God to overcome sin and darkness in and around us. (See Jesus' parable about persistent prayer, Luke 11:5–13).

"Give us today our daily bread." Bread was a daily necessity for Jesus' early followers. This request for "daily bread" put them in touch with the reality of which we all need to be reminded regularly: God's gracious provision for our daily existence. God's grace comes to us from the very beginning of the Bible's story when he creates the physical world and provides for all of the needs of Adam and Eve.

Another way to phrase this request is, "Give us what we need for today." This is very similar to the proverb which reads, "Give me neither poverty nor riches; give me only my daily bread" (Prov. 30:8b). Abundance can be dangerous to us because it can blind us to reality. Jesus knows how easy it is for us to be blinded by our self-centeredness, so he graciously gives us a God-centered prayer that works to refocus our vision.

Unless we pay close attention, we might miss the fact that Jesus instructs us to pray for our daily bread. None of us exists on our own; rather, we are born and live within a web of relationships (parents, relatives, friends, coaches, teachers, co-workers, etc.) that are necessary for our well-being. Jesus' prayer reminds us that if we are aligned with reality (the kingdom of God), we will regularly speak to our Father about the practical well-being of ourselves and others.

"Forgive us our debts as we also have forgiven our debtors." If you have a large debt that you cannot pay, receiving forgiveness of the balance by the one to whom you are indebted is good news! The Old Testament tells of a Jubilee celebration (Lev. 25–26) held every fifty years when people were forgiven all their debts, and those who had been enslaved were liberated. Jesus may have been thinking of just such a time when he taught his disciples about prayer.

Most religions believe that prayer brings us into contact with a force beyond humanity. But Jesus, in his instructions about prayer, is not teaching us to address just any god. The God that Jesus proclaims is the One who enters into our world to wipe away our debt and liberate us from the power and penalty of sin (John 3:16).

If we take the time to consider it, we will admit that we often fail to love God with our whole being and fail to love other people who are made in his image (Matt. 22:34–40). The truth is that no matter how often we have tried to be true to our calling as God's representatives on earth, we have fallen short. Our great debt means that on the final day of reckoning, we will find ourselves so far overdrawn that we will have to declare complete bankruptcy. When we ask God to forgive us our debts, we count on his being as he has revealed himself to be in Jesus. He is the "Father in heaven" who has sent his Son to wipe out our debt through his death and fill us with the Spirit who causes us to cry, "Abba, Father."

Some people are deeply troubled by Jesus' teaching about forgiveness in these verses, because he seems to base forgiveness on our having forgiven others. It is easy to see why someone would have this concern in light of Jesus' comments just a few verses later, "For if you forgive men when they sin against you, your heavenly Father will also forgive you. But if you do not forgive men their sins, your Father will not forgive your sins" (Matt. 6:14–15). This is a troubling passage that is hard to fit into the biblical notion of God's unconditional offer of forgiveness.

There is no clear resolution to this tension, but it is always helpful to look at things in light of the entire biblical story. As receivers of God's free gift of salvation in Christ, we have been radically forgiven. Likewise, we are called to be like Christ in our forgiveness of others. It seems Jesus is saying that to be his disciple is to have entered into a whole new liberating reality that is experienced through our identification with Jesus the Messiah. If we have embraced this new reality, we will be the kind of people who forgive others. If we do not extend forgiveness to others, we have not truly grasped the good news ourselves.

"Lead us not into temptation, but deliver us from the evil one." This last request zeros in on the fact that we presently experience opposition to walking in the way of the Father. Moreover, contrary to what we might assume, our Father in heaven is not first of all committed to making our life journey as easy as possible.

"Lead us not into temptation" might appear puzzling since it seems to imply that we need to request that our Father not lead us into a situation where we will be tripped up. What kind of father would be motivated by a desire to see his kids tripped up? Here we need a little understanding of the original language to make a subtle but important distinction. The word that is translated temptation (*peirasmos*) can refer to testing or to temptation—as a trap.

We know that God does not tempt us because he wants us to stumble (James 1:13), but he does sometimes lead us into and through trials as he did with Jesus when God led him, "into the wilderness to be tempted by the devil" (Matt. 4:1). Jesus, our example, prayed to be delivered from the agony of the cross but entrusted himself to the Father. Likewise, we should pray to be delivered from the testing brought about by living in an evil world; yet we should recognize that whatever God plans or allows comes from the hand of our Father in heaven.

> We want, in fact, not so much a Father in Heaven as a grandfather in heaven—a senile benevolence who, as they say, 'liked to see young people enjoying themselves', and whose plan for the universe was simply that it might be truly said at the end of each day, 'a good time was had by all.'

> —C.S. Lewis, *The Problem of Pain*[5]

In conclusion, the Jesus Prayer is centered on knowing God as Father. It also teaches us that the experiential knowledge of God as Father is a privilege that is open to all who come to him through Jesus our mediator. Jesus then teaches us that knowing God's fatherly love should motivate us to desire that the Father's goodness and greatness be known throughout the whole earth. Having experienced the blessed rule of our loving Father, we want others to experience the kindness, mercy, and love of God.

Jesus, being the truth-teller that he is, also discloses that the coming of the kingdom of God in this age does not do away with disappointments, pain, temptations, and injustices. Because of unfulfilled hunger (physical and spiritual), we are told to pray for ourselves and others, that the Father would give us today our daily bread. Because this age is also filled with sinful actions (our own and those of others), we must pray that the Father would forgive us our debts, and we must forgive others'. Finally, Jesus teaches us to recognize the providence of God in the trials we experience. Prayer is the cry of God's children who live in the tension that is created by our experience of God's fatherly care and the frustration of our human experience in this broken world. Thus it is in the context of prayer that we are made more like our Savior who taught us to pray.

NOTES

[1]Graeme Goldsworthy, *Prayer and the Knowledge of God* (Leicester, UK: InterVarsity, 2004), 10.

[2]Wayne Grudem, *Systematic Theology: An Introduction to Biblical Doctrine* (Leicester: InterVarsity Press, 1994), 376.

[3]Unless otherwise noted Scripture quotations are from the *New International Version*, 1984.

[4]Andrew Murray, *With Christ in the School of Prayer* (1895; repr., Grand Rapids: Zondervan, 1983).

[5]C.S. Lewis, *The Problem of Pain* (1944; repr., San Francisco: HarperSanFrancisco, 2001), 31.

SCRIPTURE MEMORY VERSE

Be joyful always, pray continually, give thanks in all circumstances, for this is God's will for you in Christ Jesus.
(1 Thessalonians 5:16–18 NIV)

BIBLE STUDY QUESTIONS

Matthew 6: 5–15

Jesus begins his teaching on prayer with correctives and then moves on to directives. Paying attention to both is essential for a healthy prayer life. Please read Matthew 6:5–15.

1. In his first corrective, Jesus warns against praying for public effect (vv. 5–6). What's wrong with praying to impress others?

_____

_____

_____

_____

2. Jesus also warns against repetitive and wordy prayer (v. 7). Why do you think some people feel a need to use a lot of words in repeated patterns when they pray?

_____

_____

_____

_____

3. What patterns and habits of prayer in your life might Jesus correct?

_____

_____

_____

_____

4. Since giving God new information is not the purpose of prayer (v. 8), how does this insight affect the way you should pray?

_____

_____

_____

_____

5. God knows our needs before we ask, but evidently he wants us to ask anyway. How is asking for your needs good for you?

6. The Lord's Prayer divides neatly in half, verses 9–10 and 11–13. The first half addresses the purpose, place, and character of God. In what ways are prayer (and your life) altered when God and his purposes are placed first on our prayer list?

7. Jesus invites us to address his Father as "our Father" (v. 9). How does praying to God as Jesus' Father enrich your prayers?

8. The word *heaven* is the only noun repeated twice in the prayer (vv. 9–10). How might the way we pray be enriched by our consciousness of heaven?

_____

_____

_____

_____

9. The second half of Jesus' prayer addresses our personal earthly needs: forgiveness, provision, and protection (vv. 11–13). In what way does this prayer cultivate a sense of dignity, humility, and vulnerability?

_____

_____

_____

_____

10. This prayer is not only something that we should pray, but a guideline on how we should pray. How will it be a helpful guideline for you?

_____

_____

_____

_____

GROUP DISCUSSION QUESTIONS

1. What are some ways to define Christian prayer?

   _____

   _____

2. From what you know about God, how do you think he views prayer? Why does he want to be in communication with you?

   _____

   _____

3. Do you think it is easier for a child or an adult to pray to God? Elaborate on your answer.

   _____

   _____

4. Do you find prayer to be a burdensome duty or a delight? Elaborate on your answer.

   _____

   _____

5. Do you pray with the expectation that God will answer your prayers? Why or why not?

   _____

   _____

6. What have you found to be the biggest hindrances to your prayer life? What strategies might help you overcome those prayer "bumps"?

_____

_____

7. What have you found to be the greatest encouragements to your prayer life? How can you put yourself in a position daily to receive those prayer strengtheners?

_____

_____

8. How can you use the Lord's Prayer as an outline for prayer? What are the major components of a healthy prayer life?

_____

_____

9. What are some practical steps that you can take to build a deeper daily prayer life?

_____

_____

10. Describe some different ways that you can pray during a normal day.

_____

_____

CHAPTER 9

SPEAKER BIO: JOEL S. WOODRUFF, ED.D.

VICE PRESIDENT OF DISCIPLESHIP & OUTREACH, C.S. LEWIS INSTITUTE – Joel Woodruff has worked in higher education, "tent-making," nonprofit administration, and pastoral ministries in Alaska, Israel, Hungary, France, and Northern Virginia. He served as Dean of Students, Chaplain, and Professor of Bible & Theology at European Bible Institute, where he helped train Europeans both for professional ministry and to be Christian leaders in the marketplace. Prior to joining the C.S. Lewis Institute, he was on the leadership team of Oakwood Services International, a nonprofit educational and humanitarian organization. He is a graduate of Wheaton College, earned his M.Div. from Gordon-Conwell Theological Seminary, and has a doctorate in Organizational Leadership from Nova Southeastern University. As a Parish-Pulpit Fellow, he studied Biblical Backgrounds & Archaeology in Israel for a year.

AUTHOR BIO: STEPHEN EYRE, M.DIV.

DIRECTOR, C.S. LEWIS INSTITUTE - CINCINNATI – Stephen Eyre has served both in college campus ministry and pastoral ministry for more than twenty years. He has written numerous books, Bible study guides, and devotional books that have been published nationally and internationally through Inter-Varsity Press, Zondervan, and Victor Press. Stephen has written several study guides for C.S. Lewis Institute publications including *Mere Christianity, Screwtape Letters,* and *Letters to Malcolm; Chiefly on Prayer,* as well as the Bible Study Questions for this publication. He earned a B.A. in history from Clearwater Christian College and a M.Div. from Covenant Theological Seminary.

THE MISSION OF THE CHURCH

One of the clearest directives Jesus has given us is known as the Great Commission. We read in Matthew 28:18–20 that we are to go and make disciples of all nations, baptizing them in the name of God the Father, God the Son, and God the Holy Spirit and teaching them to obey all that Jesus commanded. For the church to fulfill this important task, we must be willing to go wherever the Lord asks and serve in whatever way he directs. We're not alone in this endeavor, however, as the Lord has given us the Holy Spirit to empower and equip us to accomplish this exciting mission. There is no greater adventure on the planet than to be part of the expansion of God's kingdom on earth. The purpose of this study is to help you catch Jesus' vision for the world and to assist you in fully embracing your calling as a disciple of Jesus – to make disciples for Christ in your Jerusalem, Judea, Samaria, and to the ends of the earth.

Who doesn't want to change the world?

Funny thing: When I was in college, we thought we were a revolutionary generation and were sure that the world would be changed with our efforts—not just changed, fixed! Now I hear the same thoughts from younger generations. Evidently my generation didn't do so well on our watch.

Underlying this desire is a sense that there is something wrong. Exactly! The Christian understanding is that there is indeed something wrong. We read in Genesis that our race fell and fractured the world. It's now a fun house of mirrors that reflect distorted and even grotesque images. The world we now experience is both funny and tragic. We need a "fixer;" in religious terms, a "savior."

As Christians we believe that Jesus Christ is that "fixer/savior." Jesus, by means of his death, resurrection, and ascension, has addressed the fundamental problem, sin, and now his fixing/saving work is moving forward to consummate that renewed world in which all is as it is supposed to be.

My desire to see the world fixed—myself included—is a constantly fresh source of love for Jesus Christ and for his church. I haven't always loved the church. At one time I considered it irrelevant, old fashioned, and a source of worldwide conflict. After the summons of Jesus to believe, I discovered the church as a place of care and inspiration; I had to set aside my prejudices. Now I believe that the church is the means of changing/fixing the world, and I count it a privilege to be a part of the community and to be a part of its mission.

The word *church* brings up a variety of images, thoughts, and feelings. Perhaps you think of the church as a place where you go to worship on Sunday; perhaps it's a white colonial building with columns or a stone gothic edifice or a ramshackle wooden building out in the country. The church in which I serve was built in the sixties with jalousie windows and linoleum tile; we are currently updating it! Our church is quite nervous about the huge box church several miles away. It was once a Home Depot and has been renovated to accommodate thousands.

Maybe you think about people when you think about the church. When I look out on Sunday mornings, I see pews filled with mostly gray-haired people who wear suits or nice clothes. Our congregation is nervous about that bigger church where one sees few gray hairs and dress is casual. Maybe you have warm feelings that bring back childhood memories of Sunday school. Maybe you have bitter feelings as you think about the preacher who ran off with somebody on staff.

Whatever you see or think about when you hear the word *church*, it most likely isn't big or rich enough to accommodate God's picture and purposes for the church. If you are to take your place in God's work of changing/fixing the world, your thoughts of the church need to be stretched.

John Stott notes that:

> The church lies at the very center of the eternal purpose of God. It is not a divine afterthought. It is not an accident of history. On the contrary, the church is God's new community. For his purpose, conceived in a past eternity, being worked out in history and to be perfected in a future eternity, it is not just to save isolated individuals and so perpetuate our loneliness, but rather to build his church, that is to call out of the world a people for his own glory.[1]

What would an expanding vision of the church look like? In the book of Acts, and elsewhere in the New Testament, I see that a vision of the church includes the following themes: (1) the community of Jesus Christ, (2) the community of the Holy Spirit, (3) a missional community, (4) a redemptive community, (5) a learning community, (6) a worshiping community, and (7) a heavenly community.

THE COMMUNITY OF JESUS CHRIST

Jesus creates the church, is the center of the church, and has a purpose—a mission—for the church.

The Greek word for church is *ecclesia*. It means the "called out ones." As described in the New Testament, the church is composed of those who have been called out of the former way of life and are called into close relationship with Jesus Christ.

I used to picture the church as a huge room filled with people. Jesus was way up at the front; I could hardly see him. Everyone was facing forward and didn't even know that I had slipped into the vacant seat in the back row. It is strange that I thought that way, because it does not reflect my experience or theology. I had a clear sense of call when I entered the Faith. The first disciples were called; all that join the church thereafter are called as well (Eph. 1:4–5, 11–13). Jesus has a seat, not at the back of the church but right up front, with our name on it. It is a seat of honor. He knows we are there. He has put us there. The church is Jesus' church, and every single one of us is there for his purposes.

CHAPTER 9 – THE MISSION OF THE CHURCH

THE COMMUNITY OF THE SPIRIT

Jesus rose from the dead and for forty days taught the disciples, commissioning them to be his witnesses as the next phase of fixing/saving the world (Acts 1). Their mission was not to commence until he sent them the Holy Spirit. Jesus' gift of the Spirit to the church at the feast of Pentecost endued his church with supernatural power and gifts. Both the gifts of the Spirit and the fruit of the Spirit are present throughout the letters to the first churches (Rom. 12; 1 Cor. 12–14; Eph. 4:12–14).

Since biblical times this spiritual and supernatural nature of the church has frequently become obscured. Annie Dillard observed that on a given Sunday morning ushers pass out bulletins to sleepy people who shuffle to their seats; if people knew what the church was really about, ushers would be passing out crash helmets and life jackets!

Some churches, notably Pentecostal and charismatic, are more aware of this supernatural nature of the church than others. I am a Presbyterian, and our commitment to doing all things "decently and in order" keeps us from being eager for dramatic manifestations of the Spirit. It's a good thing that the Holy Spirit is not limited to the spontaneous and spectacular. The fruit of the Spirit—love, joy, peace, etc. (Gal. 5:22–23)—are character traits. The gifts of the Spirit include acts of compassion and mercy, teaching, and even administration. I find it interesting that two of the most Spirit-anointed people in the Scriptures were Joseph in Egypt and Daniel in Babylon, indisputably world-class administrators. We Presbyterians like that.

So is it spectacular spontaneous manifestations or orderly conduct? What really marks a church in which the Spirit is present? If we take the birth and growth of the church as our standard, it is when there is something within the church that spills out the windows and doors, flows down the street, and infects people with the life of Jesus Christ.

A MISSIONAL COMMUNITY

The arrival of the Holy Spirit brought a celestial sound and light show (Acts 2:1–13). The church's worldwide growth that began here spread throughout the Roman Empire and has continued to grow, through all of time into all cultures and languages. Jesus expected that his church would grow, and it has. Jesus, Lord of the Church, is behind it all. What amazes the people visiting Jerusalem at Pentecost was not just the sights and sounds but this: "Are not all these men who are speaking Galileans? Then how is it that each of us hears them in his own native language?" (2:7–8).[2]

The gift of the Spirit brings the reversal of the Tower of Babel, described in Genesis 11. The community of Jesus Christ, the Spirit-filled community, is the beginning of God's new society that will experience the removal of the curse—a community moving away from chaos.

The gift of the Spirit means that the message of Jesus is "translatable." The gospel can be spoken into the language, even the "heart-language," of any people group, culture, or country. This translatability means that mission of Jesus Christ doesn't need to be restricted to some authorized version, whether it be the Greek, the Latin Vulgate, the King James...

Missional is the word used since the 1990s to clarify the centrality of mission in a world that has become post-Christian. The word *missions* had been used in the nineteenth century to focus the established church beyond the horizons of Christianized Europe and America. *Mission* is what people did if they left their home country and went "over there," to darkest Africa, India, China, etc. Now that the secularized movement of the Christianized nations has resulted in "post-Christendom," the church on every block in every community is engaged in mission—not "over there" but "right here." This missional emphasis is leading to all kinds of creative and innovative ministries, some of which the more traditional churches find questionable. The missional task of the church today is moving from being a religious institution in a Christian culture to being a converting community in a post-Christian culture.

A REDEMPTIVE COMMUNITY

Peter preached his first sermon (Acts 2:14–41), and three thousand people were added to the church. The church went about incorporating those first converts and continued to grow. Their activities included the apostles' teaching, fellowship, breaking of bread, and prayer (2:42).

As a redemptive community, the church is a community of the saved. It is also a saving community. Converts experience salvation by participating in the life of the church. In spite of my many misconceptions, prejudices, and emotional needs, a little Baptist church in Florida welcomed me "home." That is, I was invited to homes for dinner and generally loved on. They taught me, nourished me, and put up with me. Immersed in their expressions of the love of God, I learned to believe, and my character began to develop. Hospitality and incorporation, then, are marks of a redemptive community. As we are engaged in mission, we not only "go and tell," but we also invite to "come and see."

CHAPTER 9 – THE MISSION OF THE CHURCH

A LEARNING COMMUNITY

The first converts "devoted themselves to the apostles' teaching" (Acts 2:42). Education is an essential ministry, as converts need to learn how to think and act as followers of Jesus Christ should; it does not come naturally. Jesus makes teaching central to mission. We see this in his Great Commission, in which he instructs disciples, "... teaching them to obey everything I have commanded you" (Matt. 28:20). The apostle Paul articulates the educational mission/ministry of the church: "Do not conform any longer to the pattern of this world, but be transformed by the renewing of your mind" (Rom. 12:2).

The church from that time to this has placed a high value on education. Those who sought to join the church attended classes twice a week for three years before they were allowed to be baptized. There were many great teachers in the first centuries of the church, Augustine of Hippo (d. 430) being the undisputed greatest. When Christianity was illegal and persecuted, one reason the church prevailed was that it "out-thought the pagans."

The high value of education of the mission/ministry of the church can be traced through the creation of the great universities and public and parochial school systems of Europe and the United States as well as the mission schools of Asia and Africa.

Our little church is attempting to recover the value of education. We have a Bible study or two available every day. The pastors' activities, which include counseling and administration, now include teaching in small groups and larger classes. In a secularizing culture, Bible illiteracy is on the rise, and there is a corresponding loss of a Christian mind and character. If the church does not excel as a learning community, we too may be secularized!

A WORSHIPING COMMUNITY

Another of the essential activities of those first converts was worship. They prayed together (Acts 2:42); they also met together in the temple courts (2:46) and even in their homes, praising God (2:47).

Worship was and remains a central focus of the church. Worshiping God is what the church does. A church wouldn't be a church if it didn't worship. The Protestant churches I am in touch with have one worship focus a week: Sunday morning with at least one service and maybe more. A few have a worship service in the evening, but not many. There are times when I envy Catholic churches in which it is common to have a daily worship service.

Worship is not generally conceived as an act of mission, but it is. We are created and converted so that we can, in the words of the Westminster Catechism, "Glorify God and enjoy him forever." During the Dark and early Middle Ages, monks and missionaries used worship as a means of reaching the Norsemen, Frisians, and uncivilized invaders. This missional aspect of worship was rediscovered by the "seeker church" in the 1980s. Sunday morning became a primary means of outreach to those drawn by the rays of the church's light.

I have been in churches where people attended worship, and I have been in churches where people worshiped. There is a difference. The way the hymns are sung, the sermon is heard, and God is engaged is noticeably different. The biblical account of the first church indicates that people were enthusiastically engaged in worship, in the temple, in the homes, in various ways. As a worshiping community was central then, it is essential now.

A Heavenly Community

While the church on earth is moving through time, it is confined to neither time nor space, for that matter. In Christ, death does not terminate life or membership in the church. In Christ, death is not a barrier nor a cul-de-sac but a bridge into another side of existence.

Robert Markus, a historian of the early church, notes that early Christians knew that:

> They were pilgrims in this world, aliens in the society of their pagan fellows, but they knew they were part of a vast community which is now traveling on its journey, to join that heavenly church … The worshiping community here on earth was an outlying colony, its prayer a distant echo of the perfect and unceasing praise offered to God in heaven by his angels and his saints. It was especially in its worship that the apparent distance between the earthly and the heavenly community was bridged.[3]

In considering the church on earth and in heaven, it is common to speak about the visible and invisible church. The visible is the church we can see; the invisible church includes those we can see and those in heaven we can't see. The church on earth is still engaged in spiritual warfare—the church militant. The church in heaven is the church triumphant. In heaven, the mission of the church is complete as it wholeheartedly enters in a worship that we have only tasted here. In an unrestrained manner they are "glorifying and enjoying God forever."

The book of Revelation gives us a glimpse of that heavenly community at worship.

> *"Day and night they never stop saying:*
>
> *'Holy, holy, holy*
> *is the Lord God Almighty*
> *who was, and is, and is to come." (4:8)*
>
> *'You are worthy, our Lord and God*
> *to receive glory and honor and power,*
> *for you created all things,*
> *and by your will they were created*
> *and have their being.'" (4:11)*

The Celtic Christians used to speak of "thin places;" that is, places where the membrane, the veil, between heaven and earth was thin, where it was possible to see and hear the sights and sounds of the heaven shining through. I have found worshiping churches to be such thin places. I hear more music than the choir makes and hear words in sermons that resonate with a depth beyond the skill of the pastor.

CONCLUSION

If we think of the church as a building, a meeting, a series of activities, or a group of people with gray or not-so-gray hair, our experience of church could be enriched if we were to expand our vision of the church to stretch back to the first believers in Acts or outward to the brothers and sisters in heaven.

We are part of a vast community that stretches through the ages and extends into eternity. We have an important role, as we are the means by which God is breaking down the barriers between heaven and earth. God is renewing and restoring his creation as we believe and obey his Son. Talk about changing the world—we get to be in the action!

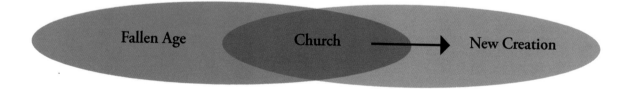

But of course there is a question: If Jesus really did fix/save the world and church is the community of the fixed/saved, then why is the world still the way it is? Wait, there is more! The church lives in the intersection of two ages. The Fallen Age has not yet been abolished, but the New Creation, the kingdom of heaven, is begun.

The church, as the agent of Jesus Christ, has the essential task to bear witness (Acts 1:8) to what is and will one day be. Saints, in the early centuries, were men and women who made the world to come seem present. At present, we are part of the church militant, and we are engaged in battles inside us, and in our culture, by forces seen and unseen. More often than we like, it seems that we are retreating rather than advancing. Despite appearances, we, the church of Jesus Christ, are God's agents for fixing/saving the world. "Even so, come, Lord Jesus"! (Rev. 22:20 KJV).

NOTES

[1]John Stott, *The Living Church* (Downers Grove, IL: InterVarsity, 2011), 19.

[2]Unless otherwise noted, Scripture quotations are from the *New International Version*, 1984.

[3]Robert Markus, *Rome to the Barbarian Kingdoms* in John McManners, ed., *The Oxford Illustrated History of Christianity* (New York: Oxford University Press, 2001), 73.

SCRIPTURE MEMORY VERSE

Then Jesus came to them and said, "All authority in heaven and on earth has been given to me. Therefore go and make disciples of all nations, baptizing them in the name of the Father and of the Son and of the Holy Spirit, and teaching them to obey everything I have commanded you. And surely I am with you always, to the very end of the age." (Matthew 28:18–20, NIV)

BIBLE STUDY QUESTIONS

Acts 2:1–47

Adam and Eve sinned, the world fractured, and God set about restoring/recreating his world. The mission of re-creation takes a major leap forward at the creation of the church in Acts. Since that day, in good times or bad, the church has never stopped growing. Read Acts 2:1–47.

1. The events on the day of Pentecost begin to fulfill Jesus' promise of church growth (Acts 1:8). What amazed those gathered in Jerusalem (2:1–12)?

_____

_____

_____

_____

2. Living in our secularizing culture, while the church has a mixed reputation, God is still at work. What is it about Christianity and the church that amazes you?

_____

_____

_____

_____

3. Peter begins his first sermon by quoting a prophet from the Old Testament (vv. 17–21). What do you see in this experience that laid the foundation for the church to be multicultural, multigenerational, and multinational?

_____

_____

_____

_____

4. In what ways could the church today learn from this Spirit-inspired "multi" vision from the prophet Joel?

_____

_____

_____

_____

5. The mission of the church is to proclaim the message: "Jesus, whom you crucified, [is] both Lord and Christ" (v. 36). What reasons does Peter offer for believing that message (vv. 22–41)?

_____

_____

_____

_____

6. Thousands responded to Peter's sermon (vv. 22–39). Why do you think his message was so convincing to the people gathered in Jerusalem?

_____

_____

_____

_____

7. How convincing is that message in our culture today? Explain.

_____

_____

_____

8. Reread verses 42–47. The church's mission and message created a fellowship. How would you describe that first fellowship of believers?

_____

_____

_____

_____

9. "The Lord added to their number daily" (v. 47). What is our role and what is God's role in the growth of the church?

_____

_____

_____

_____

10. The Holy Spirit, the gift of the Father sent by Jesus, lit the flame of mission in the fireplace of the church. What is your role in tending the flame of mission in the fireplace of the church?

_____

_____

_____

_____

GROUP DISCUSSION QUESTIONS

1. Read Matthew 28:18–20 and Acts 1:8. Look at each of the verbs in these verses and discuss how you can live out these action commands of Jesus.

2. Why is the mission of the church important to Jesus? To the church? To you, the disciple of Jesus?

3. What does the mission of the church say about God's character? His approach toward humanity?

4. What gifts has the Holy Spirit given to the church to carry out this mission?

5. Frederick Buechner writes: "The place God calls you to is the place where your deep gladness and the world's deep hunger meet." How have you seen your God-given passions connect with the needs around you?

6. Where has the Spirit used you in mission in the past? Share your experiences.

_____

_____

7. Where do you believe that you are called to serve in mission now? In the future?

_____

_____

8. How much time do I spend praying and thinking about the mission to which God has called me to?

_____

_____

9. How can you encourage other disciples, and your church, to make the mission of the church the priority that it is meant to be?

_____

_____

CHAPTER 10

SPEAKER & AUTHOR BIO: GERARD LONG

EXECUTIVE DIRECTOR, ALPHA USA – Following a dramatic encounter with God in 1980, Gerard felt a calling to serve in a church in North London. He was at this church for twenty-two years, including seventeen as a pastor, while also working in the banking and finance industry. Gerard has a BSc (Hons) Banking and Finance degree and worked for HSBC (one of the largest banks in the world) for thirty years, retiring at the end of 2006 as Senior Vice President, Corporate Marketing. In 2006, Gerard decided to leave behind his highly paid banking career and join Alpha USA, whose mission is to serve local churches in presenting the gospel through the Alpha course. Alpha is now being run in over 169 countries and more than 15 million people have gone through the course. Gerard lives with his wife, Jeannie, in Lake Forest, Illinois, and has two children, Rebecca and Ben.

SHARING THE GOOD NEWS

The word gospel, *means "good news." Again and again we read in the New Testament the importance of proclaiming the gospel, preaching the gospel, and not being ashamed of the gospel of Jesus Christ. The first four books of our New Testament are called "Gospels" because they tell the good news of the birth, life, death, and resurrection of Jesus. As Christ's disciples, we have the most amazing story in the world to share with those around us. That's really what evangelism is about—telling others the story of Christ and giving them the opportunity to receive the free gift of salvation by grace through faith in Christ. And yet, most of us find that evangelism can be a difficult thing to do. The intent of this study is to help you understand how to be God's mouthpiece as you share the good news, by the power of the Holy Spirit, with your neighbors, family, and even your enemies.*

THE HEART OF THE GOSPEL

When God sent his Son Jesus Christ into the world, he didn't do it to condemn the world but to save the world through him (John 3:17). Jesus came to rescue precious souls from sin and death and to bring us hope and a future. The name Jesus means Savior, and he was totally successful in his mission!

To evangelize simply means to share "good news." From the Greek word *evangelize* we get the word *angel*, which means messenger. When the angel announced the birth of Jesus to the shepherds on that first Christmas, he came to evangelize them: "Do not be afraid. I bring you good news of great joy that will be for all the people. Today in the town of David a Savior has been born for you; he is Christ the Lord" (Luke 2:10–11).[1]

In the Great Commission, Jesus called every disciple to share the Good News of Jesus Christ: "Therefore go and make disciples of all nations, baptizing them in the name of the Father and of the Son and of the Holy Spirit, and teaching them to obey everything I have commanded you. And surely I am with you always, to the very end of the age" (Matt. 28:19–20).

Early in his ministry Jesus said, "Follow me [a disciple is a Christ follower], and I will make you fishers of men" (Matt. 4:19). From this we see that the end result of discipleship is to be a fisher of one's fellowmen. Later in the New Testament we see that all Christ followers have been equipped through the Holy Spirit to be witnesses of Jesus Christ (Acts 1:8) and to be his ambassadors here on earth (2 Cor. 5:20).

When we have good news—whether it's about an amazing person we've met, a new job, a new home, or an incredible vacation we've just had, we don't have to be encouraged to tell our family and friends. We all like to share good news, and, if it's well received, it encourages our hearers.

Throughout the Gospels, when people met Jesus Christ, they told other people about him. Think of the Samaritan woman at the well in John 4. We're told many people believed because the woman shared what she'd seen, heard, and experienced—the transforming power of Jesus. In the book of Acts, starting with the 120 disciples in the Upper Room, the early disciples turned the world "upside down" through evangelization—sharing the Good News of Jesus Christ.

Today we need to learn afresh how to evangelize. A recent Barna study showed that only 3 percent of sixteen- to twenty-nine-year-olds have a positive view of evangelical Christians! Instead of drawing people to Jesus, we've turned them away from him!

Sharing the Good News of Jesus Christ should not be something we dread. It can be something we love to do, flowing naturally from the power of the Holy Spirit in our lives. Where do we start a vital evangelism campaign for and in America? I suggest we ask God to renew our vision, faith, courage, and action.

Lord, Renew Our Vision

Lord, I pray, renew our vision of your love for us and for the lost. But there's more to this prayer: Lord, give us a clearer understanding of your eternal purpose and plan.

God's Love for the Human Race

Here's the Good News: "For God so loved the world that he gave his one and only Son, that whoever believes in him shall not perish but have eternal life" (John 3:16). God doesn't want anyone to perish but all to come to repentance (2 Pet. 3:9). God has "reconciled us to himself through Christ," and he has entrusted to Christ followers this amazing message of reconciliation (2 Cor. 5:18). In the first few chapters of Acts, God has given us a model of how this love and power works in practice.

In Acts 1 we see 120 disciples hidden away in an upper room. They knew they had been commissioned to be witnesses of the resurrection, but they had no power or vision. Then, as recorded in Acts 2, the Holy Spirit came and filled them—changing everything. They were empowered and transformed to do extraordinary things, and these people turned the world upside down (Acts 17:6). Just think, it started with only 120 disciples! How did this happen? I believe there are two keys.

First, in Acts 2 we witness Pentecost when the disciples were filled with the Holy Spirit. From that moment on, the disciples began to evangelize the world with the message of redemption through Jesus Christ.

Born into a wonderful Christian family, I came to faith in Christ when I was very young. I certainly had the Holy Spirit, but I was not *filled* with the Holy Spirit. That happened on February 14, 1980, in a powerful encounter with God. I was dramatically transformed and fell head over heels in love with Jesus Christ, so much so that I only wanted to please and glorify him. Also the Bible came alive to me. I couldn't put it down, and I desperately wanted to evangelize my friends! I was filled with the Holy Spirit, and since then I have been filled again and again and again (Eph 5:18). As D.L. Moody said, "I need to keep on being filled with the Holy Spirit because I leak!"

It's the Holy Spirit who pours God's love into our hearts (Rom. 5:5), and this love compels us to lay down our lives in order to carry out the mission (2 Cor. 5:14–15). And it's the Holy Spirit who empowers us to be witnesses of the Good News of Jesus Christ to lost and broken people (Acts 1:8).

As Christ followers, we desperately need to ask God to keep on filling us with the Holy Spirit (Luke 11:9–13). As Billy Graham said, "It's not an option for a Christian to be filled with the Holy Spirit; it's a necessity."

God's Plan of Redemption

The Holy Spirit also helps us to understand God's bigger picture of redemption. This, I believe, is the second key that will help Christ followers to evangelize the world. Relative to eternity, our lives on earth are but a breath or a vapor (Ps. 39:5), but, while we are on earth, God has called us to complete a specific mission. To be effective in completing the work God has set for each of us (Eph. 2:10), we're called to live as aliens and strangers on earth (1 Pet. 2:11). And our faithfulness to the work he has given us will be rewarded *through eternity* (2 Cor. 5:10).

God has enabled me to understand this bigger picture through the demise of close family members. Through the brokenness caused by the death of my youngest son Alex in 2005, followed two months later by the death of my sister Jax, eternity has become very real to me. Scripture says God has "set eternity in the hearts of men" (Eccl. 3:11), and often brokenness will release this understanding. While it is certainly true that God wants us to glorify him by living abundant lives here and now, we do that by having our eyes and hearts fixed on eternal things (2 Cor. 4:18), on the things above (Col. 3:1–3). Moses prayed, "Teach us to number our days aright, that we may gain a heart of wisdom" (Ps. 90:12). Having an eternal perspective helps us to set correct priorities for our days on earth.

C.S. Lewis said:

> If you read history, you will find that the Christians who did the most for the present world were just those who thought most of the next. The Apostles themselves, Wilberforce and the English Evangelicals who abolished the slave trade, all left their mark on Earth, precisely because their minds were occupied with heaven. It is since Christians have largely ceased to think of the other world that they have become so ineffective in this. Aim at Heaven and you will get earth thrown in; aim at earth and you will get neither.[2]

In Acts 3 and Acts 4, we see how this perspective influenced the actions of the early disciples. In Acts 3 a man who has been crippled for forty years is healed in Jesus' name as Peter and John are going into the temple. The city is in uproar on account of this healing, and Peter and John are dragged before the religious leaders. In Acts 4, I note some key statements. In verse 12 we're told that salvation comes only through Jesus Christ, and in verse 13 we're informed that evangelization can come through uneducated, ordinary people who know Jesus! *By God's grace and the power of the Holy Spirit, everybody can and should be evangelizing!*

In Acts 4:18 the religious leaders basically say to Peter and John, "Look, unless you stop speaking about Jesus Christ, we're going to kill you." And in verse 20, they respond with these amazing words, "We cannot help speaking about what we have seen and heard." Again, to paraphrase, they're saying, "Kill us if you want, but what we've seen and heard is so incredible that we have to share it with other people, even if it means our losing our lives in the process!"

What did they see and hear that they were willing to die for? Well, we know that they saw and walked with Jesus on earth. They saw how he lived. They saw his example; they heard and saw what the kingdom of God looked like. They also saw Jesus die on the cross, and they saw him alive again in his resurrected body. They saw that life does not end when our physical bodies die; there is much more to come! And of course they heard all that Jesus had spoken when he was with them. He spoke about the kingdom of God, and he also spoke a lot about the afterlife. He spoke about heaven, and he spoke about hell.

Regrettably, we've got to a place in our society where we don't want to hear about hell. It's uncomfortable and not "politically correct." Whatever we feel about hell, the key question is, what is the truth? Do we believe Jesus was telling the truth when he warned people about eternal judgment? If we believe hell is a reality, it should fundamentally change how we go about our lives. If we know the end of the story, and other people don't, I think it's fair to say that we've got an obligation to tell them about it. *Not out of guilt, but out of a genuine concern and compassion for people, deep in our hearts.* If a blind man was about to walk off a cliff, how hard would we try to persuade him to change course? If he's convinced he's on the right path, we'd have to be strategic in how we persuaded him to take another course.

I believe God wants to give Christ followers a fresh and clear vision of his calling on our lives. When he told Joshua to go in and take the Promised Land, God gave him a clear vision. He defined the area of land to take and told him what he would need to carry out the task.

The Bible says, "Without a vision the people perish" (Prov. 29:18, KJV). What is your vision for your life? Why are you living here on earth (assuming you are living)?

I heard about an old man who was asked what he did first thing in the morning. He said, "The first thing I do in the morning is read the obituaries in the *New York Times*. If I'm not in it, I get up to face a new day!" What do you get up to do each morning?

Maybe a better question is, what is God's will for you here on earth? After all, as Christ followers, we're called to live for God's will, right? Our fulfillment is to do God's will.

The kingdom of God will break out across America if the church is renewed and Christ followers are mobilized once again to evangelize the lost and perishing: friends, neighbors, relatives, and work colleagues.

What is your vision to obey the Great Commission, to make disciples of all nations? What are you doing about the people whom God has put in your life?

Jesus clarified and confirmed his mission on earth when he said, "For the Son of Man came to seek and to save what was lost" (Luke 19:10). And he says to us, "As the Father has sent me, I am sending you" (John 20:21).

FAITH

The second area that needs renewal is our faith. Faith comes from hearing the message and the message is heard through the word of Christ (Rom. 10:17). As we hear God's message and heart for the lost through Scripture, faith is stirred in our hearts. And faith leads to victory! (1 John 5:4).

The big question is, are we really hearing the message? When asked what God requires, Jesus replied, "The work of God is this: to believe in the one he has sent" (John 6:29). Do we believe enough in the things we have seen and heard that we would die in order to tell them to other people?

Mohammed was an Iraqi Muslim who came to faith in Christ. The gospel so impacted his life that he felt compelled to share the Good News with his family. "I have happiness; I cannot stop myself," he told his wife Liyla. "I must share this truth with my family." But his words were not received well, and a family member murdered him for leaving the Islamic faith. Widowed and with a young child to care for, his young wife was encouraged to flee Iraq along with other Christians. But Liyla decided to stay and witness about Jesus Christ for whom her husband had given his life. As a result of her faith and courage, other Muslim women are coming to faith in Christ![3]

There is an amazing YouTube clip of a magician named Penn, who shares how impressed he was by a man who gave him a New Testament and Psalms. He goes on say that although he is an atheist, he has never had a problem with Christians proselytizing because, "If they believe what they say about heaven and hell, why aren't they telling us more about them?" And, of course, he has a great point. Not that Christians should go about telling people they're going to hell (that rarely works!), but we should be more active in sharing the Good News about Jesus Christ our Savior.

Scripture clearly indicates that the evidence of our faith will be seen by how we live and what we do (John 14:21, 23; James 2:22). Again, this comes through the work of the Holy Spirit. We need to keep asking him to fill us with his love and power, enabling us to be witnesses for Christ (Eph. 5:18).

COURAGE

I also challenge you to ask God, by the power of the Holy Spirit, to renew your courage. When commanding Joshua to take the land they had been given, God told him three times to "be strong and very courageous!"

Courage is not the absence of fear or pain but a willingness to do what is right whatever the cost. Jesus modeled this perfectly on the Mount of Olives just before his crucifixion. Aware of what was coming, he was in mental and emotional agony, so much so that he started to sweat blood. He cried out, "Father, if you are willing, take this cup from me; yet not my will, but yours be done" (Luke 22:42). This is a total surrender of his will to the will of God.

CHAPTER 10 – SHARING THE GOOD NEWS

To obey God's Great Commission to evangelize requires courage and involves sacrifice as priorities shift and we focus our time and energy on following Christ and becoming fishers of men. What's more, an enemy scheming against us has come to kill, rob, and destroy (John 10:10). Praise God, we do have the victory in Christ, but we need to recognize and engage in the battle. As Paul said to Timothy, we need to have the attitude of a soldier, athlete, and farmer (2 Tim. 2:1–7).

"For our struggle is not against flesh and blood, but against the rulers, against the authorities, against the powers of this dark world and against the spiritual forces of evil in the heavenly realms" (Eph. 6:12).

And all the sacrifice is more than worth it both today and through eternity. When the church fails to obey the Great Commission, Satan and the spiritual forces of evil in the heavenly realms go unopposed, thereby causing darkness in and confusion over every societal arena, including politics, the economy, morality, and the media. But when the church obeys Jesus' instructions to go and evangelize, to share the Good News about him and the kingdom of God, Satan is displaced from the heavenly realm. This leads to the kingdom of God breaking out in every area of society.

ACTION

In 1865 William Booth had a vision from God in which he saw a raging sea with masses of perishing souls in the water. Then he saw a huge rock with a platform rising out of the water, and some of the people were being saved from the raging sea. But his heart broke because so few people who had been saved from drowning had any concern for those who were still perishing! From this vision, Booth started the Salvation Army.

We need renewal in a fourth and final aspect: in simply taking action. It's so easy to just hear the message and then do nothing about it.

I love the film *Schindler's List*, in particular, the powerful ending, when Schindler—who has risked his life to save so many Jews in the Holocaust—realizes after the war that he could have done more. He could have saved more victims from the gas chambers! Will there be a time, I wonder, when this age has come to an end, and we realize we could have done more to evangelize the lost?

NOTES

[1]Unless otherwise noted, Scripture quotations are from the *New International Version*, 1984.

[2]C.S. Lewis, *Mere Christianity* ((New York: Simon & Schuster/Touchtone, 1996), 119

[3]Voice of the Martyrs, September 2011.

SCRIPTURE MEMORY VERSE

But you will receive power when the Holy Spirit comes on you; and you will be my witnesses in Jerusalem, and in all Judea and Samaria, and to the ends of the earth. (Acts 1:8, NIV)

BIBLE STUDY QUESTIONS

Matthew 28:1–20

The last chapter of Matthew focuses on messengers of Jesus' resurrection—the angel tells the women, the women tell the disciples, the disciples tell the nations, and even the guards tell the religious leaders. Please read Matthew 28.

1. In the beginning of Jesus' ministry, John the Baptist prepared the way. Now, after the resurrection, the angel prepares the way (vv. 2–7). In what ways is a messenger, or witness, helpful in preparing for faith in Christ?

_____

_____

_____

_____

2. Some people come to faith as they grow up; others come to faith after childhood. Either way, there were people who were messengers, or "witnesses," to you. Who have been your significant witnesses, and what did they do to encourage you to believe?

_____

_____

_____

_____

3. The leaders circulated a rumor that the disciples stole the body to keep people from believing in Jesus (vv. 11–15). What keeps people today from believing that Jesus is the resurrected Lord?

_____

_____

_____

_____

4. The disciples go to Galilee, where they meet with Jesus. How was the experience of three disciples at the Mount of Transfiguration (Matt. 16:28–17:9) confirmed and expanded on the Mount of Resurrection?

_____

_____

_____

_____

5. What confirms, affirms, and encourages you to believe the message of Jesus enough to share it with others?

_____

_____

_____

_____

6. In Matthew 28:16–20, Jesus gave to the disciples what we now call the Great Commission. Describe the commission he gives to them and us.

Make disciples of all nations — Baptizing them in the name of the Father, Son, & Holy Spirit & teaching them to obey all commands of Jesus — I am with you always

7. How would this commission have sounded to the Jewish disciples? How does it sound to you?

_____

_____

_____

_____

8. The mission on which Jesus sends the disciples calls for baptizing in the name of the triune God: the Father, the Son, and the Holy Spirit (v. 19). What are you asking people to believe when you invite them into the Christian faith?

_____

_____

_____

_____

9. Baptizing (v. 19) is a rite or an act of confirmation and incorporation into the Christian community. What role does the church, as the community of Christ, have in the task of evangelism?

_____

_____

_____

_____

10. Some see verses 16–20 as indicating that the entire Gospel of Matthew was written as a manual for fulfilling Jesus' command to evangelize, teach, and disciple. What can you do to use the Gospel of Matthew, and the other three Gospels, to empower and encourage you in fulfilling Jesus' Great Commission?

_____

_____

_____

_____

Group Discussion Questions

1. What means did God use to communicate the good news of Jesus with you for the first time?

    _____

    _____

2. Describe some things that get you excited when thinking about all that God has done for you.

    _____

    _____

3. When you hear the word *evangelism*, what thoughts or ideas come to mind? Be honest and share both negative and positive images?

    _____

    _____

4. What hinders you from sharing the good news of Christ with your neighbors, your family, and others?

    _____

    _____

5. What helps you not to be ashamed of the gospel and gives you boldness to share your faith?

    _____

    _____

6. What part does the Holy Spirit play as you share your faith with others? How does this change the way you may think about evangelism?

_____

_____

7. What practices could you integrate into your life to make evangelism just a part of your normal life?

_____

_____

8. Share some examples of how you have been able to share the good news of Jesus Christ with others.

_____

_____

NOTES TO LEADERS

Why lead the *Heart and Mind Discipleship* program?

Would you like to help other believers become more effective witnesses for Jesus Christ in their personal and public spheres? To see your friends become more active in the church and excited about their faith? Would you also like to follow Jesus more intently in thought, word, and deed, allowing him to work in both your heart and mind?

If your answer is yes, we at the C.S. Lewis Institute encourage you to lead a small group through this *Heart and Mind Discipleship* program. We believe you will be thrilled at the results that take place in your life and the lives of others. The dynamics will only partially depend on the great teaching, thoughtful reading, Bible studies, and group discussion offered through the program. In large part, the growth in your spiritual life and others' will be due to your leadership as you cooperate with the Wonderful Counselor himself, the Holy Spirit.

The *Heart and Mind Discipleship* package provides you with all of the essential components needed for a ten-week, life-impacting study on Christian discipleship. Of course the hope is that after the ten weeks you and your friends will want to continue to deepen your relationship with Christ in the forthcoming days, months and years.

The thirty-minute DVD lectures are taught by a variety of experienced teachers and focus on key discipleship themes. For each weekly theme, group participants will read a short article in the workbook, complete a short Bible study, and then meet as a group to hear the thirty-minute lecture. Discussion questions are provided for the leader and the group to consider after hearing the lecture.

By reading, studying, listening to, and then discussing the session theme, learners are able to absorb the material in a variety of ways. One person might resonate with the lecture; another might note something in the reading. This approach to the study helps people glean insights from one another. The cumulative effect is that group members should not only learn more about Christ, but also become better equipped to live out their faith in daily life.

This program could be used in a home group, as a curriculum for your church's small group program, in an adult Sunday school class, or in a workplace environment given the right circumstances, such as with a weekly lunch or breakfast group.

What do C.S. Lewis and the C.S. Lewis Institute have to do with discipleship?

Founded in 1976 in the legacy of C.S. Lewis, the Institute endeavors to develop disciples who can articulate, defend, and live faith in Christ through personal and public living. Over the years, the C.S. Lewis Institute has seen the critical role that small groups play in helping people mature in their Christian faith. Small groups play a key role in CSLI programs as believers are able to encourage, teach, exhort, and enjoy one another in community.

A case in point is C.S. Lewis himself, who saw the importance of studying together with other like-minded people. He developed his critical-thinking skills in his teens under the tutelage of W.T. Kirkpatrick, "the great Knock." As Lewis was forced to dialogue back and forth on a topic, he sharpened his mind and absorbed the teaching. Later Lewis would apply this to his students, when he tutored small groups at Oxford and Cambridge. He also learned the invaluable role of friends in search of truth. In small group gatherings and one-on-one conversations with writers such as J.R.R. Tolkien, Charles Williams, and Owen Barfield, he eventually came to faith in Christ.

Once he was a believer, Lewis and other gifted writers polished their works in a weekly small group called the Inklings. Out of this small group came literary works of extraordinary power and impact for Christ, including *The Chronicles of Narnia*, by Lewis, and *The Lord of the Rings*, by Tolkien. These books were hammered out as the group read their works aloud, critiquing and helping one another craft better stories.

During World War II, Lewis was asked to give radio broadcasts on Christianity to Britain. Lewis was the second-best-known radio voice of the war years, just behind the great prime minister Winston Churchill. These radio talks led to the eventual publishing of Lewis's *Mere Christianity*.

Through these life experiences and his deep understanding of the New Testament, C.S. Lewis came to see how a combination of the written word, the spoken word, small group discussions, and one-on-one tutoring or mentoring can lead one into a deeper relationship with Jesus Christ.

The example of Jesus Christ as small group discipleship leader:

One of the first things Jesus did to start his ministry was recruit a small group of disciples. We read in Mark 3:13–14 (NIV), "Jesus went up on a mountainside and called to him those he wanted, and they came to him. He appointed twelve—designating them apostles—that they might be with him and that he might send them out to preach."

Jesus set out to create a small group of men who would be able to minister to one another and the world. Jesus understood small group dynamics and formed his group sizes to match his purposes. Modern research in the fields of psychology and sociology has shown that:

- *Twelve* in a group is the maximum size for effective teaching with a small group dynamic, not including the leader which makes thirteen, total.

- *Four* in a group provide an ideal size for deeper sharing, discussions, and relationships. The problem with a group of three is that it can become a two-versus-one scenario. (Peter, James, John, and Jesus made up a group of four that experienced significant events together, such as the Transfiguration, and the night in the Garden of Gethsemane.)

- *Two* is the ideal pairing for sharing one's deepest experiences and questions. This size is best for confession and intimate sharing. (Jesus and John formed this group of two. John was tasked with caring for Jesus' personal affairs following his death and caring for his mother, Mary, as a result of their close relationship.) Also note that Jesus sent the disciples out two by two for mutual support. He never sent his disciples out alone.

Following Jesus' resurrection and just before his ascension, he commissioned the small group of apostles by saying to them, "All authority in heaven and on earth has been given to me. Therefore go and make disciples of all nations, baptizing them in the name of the Father and the Son and the Holy Spirit, and teaching them to obey everything I have commanded you" (Matt. 28:18–20, NIV).

It is this small group of apostles that ended up "turning the world upside down." As they depended on the power of the Holy Spirit, they spread the good news of Christ throughout the Roman Empire.

In Acts 2:42–47 we read of a number of different disciplines or practices that characterized the early church, including:

1. Teaching
2. Fellowship
3. Breaking of Bread (Lord's Supper)
4. Prayer & Worship
5. Healing, Wonders, Miraculous Signs
6. Caring for One Another
7. Assimilating New People into the Church

We discover that while teaching, prayer and worship, and healing took place in their large gatherings, all of the characteristics of the early church were practiced in small groups that met in homes throughout the week. In other words, home groups or small groups were the primary means of living out one's faith and becoming a mature disciple of Christ. Unfortunately, many in the church today who attend only a Sunday morning service miss out on the power that comes from being involved with a small group of believers who are seeking the Lord together so that they can better fulfill Christ's great commission.

Professor Roberta Hestenes provides a good definition of what a *Heart and Mind Discipleship* group intends to be: "A Christian small group is an intentional, face-to-face gathering of 3–12 people on a regular time schedule with a common purpose of discovering and growing in the possibilities of the abundant life in Christ."

The role and responsibilities of the *Heart and Mind Discipleship* group leader:

1. P-L-A-N. Before you begin, take time to plan by reading this leadership guide and the study guide introduction to the program. Then begin the steps of planning:

urpose. Know the purpose of the *Heart and Mind Discipleship* program: that you and your friends will experience authentic spiritual growth as you seek to learn how to become more mature disciples of Jesus Christ. Determine how you can best communicate the purpose of this small group discipleship program to the people you intend to invite to participate.

ogistics. Determine the logistics of:

When: When will you meet (date, time, for how long)?

Where: Where will you meet (home, church, workplace)?

What: What will you need to do to prepare the place for the weekly meetings (seating, lighting, TV/DVD player, room temperature, beverages, snacks, childcare, removal of distractions)?

Who: Who will take care of the various planning pieces? Don't be afraid to delegate. People like to contribute and actually become more committed when they play a role in the group, even if it's just preparing refreshments or setting up chairs.

Some possible roles include:

Leader
Assistant Leader
Hospitality Coordinator
Technology Coordinator (TV/DVD)
Childcare Coordinator
Facilities Coordinator

ctivities. The *Heart and Mind Discipleship* program has a suggested activity plan for different types of groups. If your group has time to meet for a meal or even dessert, the fellowship over food can help build relationships and thus enhance the overall experience. Below are a few suggested formats. The 90- to 120-minute weekly sessions are the ideal. If time is of the essence, a 60-minute session can be used, although it allows a lot less time for group discussion.

SAMPLE SMALL GROUP STUDY AGENDA (TOTAL: 90 MINUTES)	
10 Minutes	Social Time
5 Minutes	Introduction of Topic and Prayer
30 Minutes	Play DVD Teaching
35 Minutes	Discussion Questions
10 Minutes	Closing: Recite Memory Verse & Prayer Time

HOME GROUP DINNER AND STUDY MODEL (TOTAL: 120 MINUTES)	
40 Minutes	Simple Dinner and Social Time (Pizza, Salad, Drinks, and Desserts—or a potluck)
5 Minutes	Introduction of Topic and Prayer
30 Minutes	Play DVD Teaching
35 Minutes	Discussion Questions
10 Minutes	Closing: Recite Memory Verse & Prayer Time

SUNDAY SCHOOL CLASS/ WORKPLACE MODEL	
5 Minutes	Introduction of Topic and Prayer
30 Minutes	Play DVD Teaching
25–55 Minutes	Discussion Questions, Memory Verse & Prayer Time

Take some time each week to plan out the activities for the meeting so that things flow smoothly. **Always start and end on time.** People will get discouraged if the meetings go overtime or start late. If you desire, you can end the formal meeting on time and give people the option to stay later to fellowship or pray more. But always give people the opportunity to end at the prescheduled times.

Needs. Be on the alert to the needs of the people who are either in the group or may join the group. As you pray and ask the Holy Spirit to guide your planning process, he will give you guidance and help you determine the needs of your particular group and your responsibilities in meeting those needs.

Rick Howerton, in his book *Destination Community*, suggests some key questions to ask the Lord each week to prepare for small group leadership:

> **Is there:** Someone to pray with?
> Someone needing counsel?
> Someone to encourage?
> Someone to hold accountable?
> Something to celebrate with someone?
> Something to learn?
> A need to be met?
> A call to be made?
> A conflict to be resolved?

2. Pray and recruit participants. After planning, the second task of the leader is to pray and recruit the participants. Take some time to pray and ask the Lord to lead and point you to the right people to be in the study. The series is not intended to be evangelistic, though new believers would be well served by the content, as well as those who have been Christians for a long time. Then begin inviting. Don't be disappointed if some say, "No, thank you." Persevere and keep on inviting until you get a committed small group together.

Jim Collins, author of the modern leadership bestseller *Good to Great*, writes, "Great endeavors are accomplished best when the right people are in the right place doing the right thing." As you pray and ask the Lord to put together the right group, have faith that he can arrange the right people in the right place doing the right thing.

A personal invitation or a phone call is the preferred method of communication, as an impersonal e-mail might be overlooked and does not provide immediate conversational answers to questions.

Bobb Biehl gives the following advice in his book *Mentoring*:

> "Don't hesitate—initiate."

You should be prepared to answer the following questions when recruiting people for the study. You might try to formulate an honest answer that you would like to hear if you were considering a study.

Be prepared to answer the following questions when recruiting a potential disciple:

1. How much time each week will it take for me to prepare for and do the study?
2. How long will the study last?
3. What kind of homework is involved?
4. Does it cost anything?
5. Do you have to know a lot of Bible or be able to pray out loud to be in the group?
6. How many people will be in the group?
7. What are we going to do in the meetings?
8. Who else is coming?
9. Do you provide childcare?
10. Can I leave midway through the study if I find it's just not for me?

Group size: While a larger group could watch the DVD teaching together, it is recommended that discussion groups be small. It is hard to have interactive discussions with groups larger than thirteen including the discussion facilitator.

3. Develop a group covenant. Covenants provide a means of providing purpose, balance, and accountability within small group relationships. If people have knowingly signed a covenant, they are more likely to follow through on their commitment. What's more, the covenant makes it easier for people to give grace and/or lovingly confront someone who is not living up to the covenant.

For example, if someone is regularly missing the group's meetings, the leader of the group can say, "Hey, we've missed you recently. Your contribution is important and necessary for our group to function and grow. What can we do to help you make it to the group next week and fulfill your covenant?"

One of the first things a group can do to assure success is to agree upon a covenant. A covenant needs to take into consideration both the principles and logistics needed to achieve the group's goal. It would be wise to write up your covenant and then distribute copies to everyone in the group. Have the group discuss it and express any concerns or reservations about it. It can be adapted to meet the needs of the group as long as it doesn't compromise the mission of the program.

Some of the key components might include:

Attendance: a commitment to attend the weekly meetings for the ten-week period barring an unexpected emergency.

Preparation: a commitment to do the homework and to come prepared to the meetings. However, if participants haven't finished the homework, they should be encouraged to come anyway so that they can benefit from the group's discussion and get back on track.

Prayer: a commitment to pray for the group and that the Holy Spirit would help everyone grow spiritually through all the components of the program.

Confidentiality: anything shared in the group must stay in the group and not be shared with others. This is an important part of the covenant as it builds trust when maintained and allows people to be more open.

Openness: a willingness to share and participate in the discussions.

Honesty: a commitment to being honest and forthright in all relationships within the group.

Sensitivity: a commitment to being sensitive to the needs of others in the group.

Love: a commitment to love those in the group as commanded by Christ himself.

4. **Facilitate discussion.** The great thing about the *Heart and Mind Discipleship* program is that you don't have to be a theologian or biblical scholar to lead this study. All you need is to be a committed follower of Jesus Christ who wants to grow spiritually and wants to bring people alongside to grow as well. Most of the programming is already done for you. Having said that, you will be asked to facilitate the group discussion. Discussion questions are provided to help you. These questions can be modified, adapted, or you can use some questions of your own to get people talking. The key is to get others talking rather than doing the talking yourself.

An **"ask, don't tell"** policy is a good approach when leading the thematic discussion. Usually people should be ready to talk after watching the DVD, having read the article, and having completed the Bible study in preparation for the group time.

Some things to remember:

- Remember the questions who? what? when? where? why? and how?

- Give people time to answer. Don't answer your own question. Rephrase it if you'd like, but don't be afraid of "pregnant pauses." Someone might be ready to birth an amazing response, but it takes time sometimes.

- Be affirming by using expressions such as, "Great insight," "You're on the right track; can you expand on that?" or "Wow!"

- Repeat responses as a way to get people to continue talking.

- Don't ask yes/no questions. If you do, have people expand their answers.

- Redirect people if they start to get off track. It's alright to politely interrupt and ask them to get back to the question or the main idea of the conversation.

- Don't go off on rabbit trails—topics outside of the focus of the meeting.

- Don't let one person dominate the conversation. Politely ask to hear from others in the group.

5. **Start and end on time.** This point was stated earlier but is crucial to maintaining the morale of your group. If you meet the expectations of your group when it comes to the beginning and ending time of your meeting, you'll be trusted with other things later on. Be trustworthy in the little things, such as timing, and people will begin to trust you on more important matters. People live busy lives and need to know that they'll be dismissed on time. If you go late, you may lose people in future meetings. Also start on time, cluing people to the importance of arriving on time. If people know you'll be starting late, they will begin arriving late; it's just human nature.

6. **Model what it takes to grow from the study by preparing yourself each week for the group study.** In other words, practice what you preach and complete the Bible study, reading, and memorization assignment each week.

7. **Use the leadership guide and study guide resources.** If you find that you have a question about the study to which an answer can't be found in the materials, feel free to contact the C.S. Lewis Institute. The website of CSLI is www.cslewisinstitute.org

8. **Pray and enjoy the program!** Pray for the members of your group and pray that the Holy Spirit would guide the discussion. Pray that all distractions would be removed during the meeting. Do the work, show up to the group, facilitate the discussion, get to know the people in your group, and enjoy the program!

ADDITIONAL RESOURCES

BOOKS ON CHRISTIAN ESSENTIALS

Mere Christianity, C.S. Lewis

Basic Christianity, John R.W. Stott

The Reason for God, Tim Keller

Searching Issues, Nicky Gumbel

Jesus Among Other Gods, Ravi Zacharias

ARTICLES AND BOOKS ON THE THEMES OF HEART AND MIND DISCIPLESHIP

1) God's Character & Personality

"Four Circles of Intimacy with God," by J. Oswald Sanders. *Knowing & Doing*, C.S. Lewis Institute, Fall 2006. http://www.cslewisinstitute.org/webfm_send/517

"The Holiness of God," by Dr. Art Lindsley. *Knowing & Doing*, C.S. Lewis Institute, Fall 2008. http://www.cslewisinstitute.org/webfm_send/542

In His Image, Michael Wilkins

The Pursuit of God, A. W. Tozer

2) God's Story of Redemption

"Creation, Fall, Redemption," by Dr. Art Lindsley. *Knowing & Doing*, C.S. Lewis Institute, Winter 2009. http://www.cslewisinstitute.org/webfm_send/409

3) Understanding Salvation

"Is Jesus the Only Way to God?," by Dennis Hollinger. *Knowing & Doing*, C.S. Lewis Institute, Spring 2009. http://www.cslewisinstitute.org/webfm_send/564

Why Jesus?, Ravi Zacharias

4) God's Plan for Our Growth

"10 Questions to Ask to Make Sure You're Still Growing," by Donald Whitney. *Knowing & Doing*, C.S. Lewis Institute, Winter 2007. http://www.cslewisinstitute.org/webfm_send/497

"Maturity Can be Measured," by Oswand Sanders. *Knowing & Doing*, C.S. Lewis Institute, Winter 2005. http://www.cslewisinstitute.org/webfm_send/627

Transforming Grace, Jerry Bridges

5) The Cost of Discipleship

"The Call to Discipleship," by Tim Keller. *Knowing & Doing*, C.S. Lewis Institute, Special Discipleship Issue. Winter 2011. http://www.cslewisinstitute.org/webfm_send/887

"The Transforming Impact of True Discipleship," by Tom Tarrants. *Knowing & Doing*, C.S. Lewis Institute, Special Discipleship Issue. Spring 2011. http://www.cslewisinstitute.org/webfm_send/246

"The Discipleship Deficit," by Greg Ogden. *Knowing & Doing*, C.S. Lewis Institute, Special Discipleship Issue. Spring 2011. http://www.cslewisinstitute.org/webfm_send/236

The Cost of Discipleship, Dietrich Bonhoeffer

Radical, David Platt

6a) Humility & Servanthood

"To Increase Humility," by Jeremy Taylor. *Knowing & Doing*, C.S. Lewis Institute, Winter 2009. http://www.cslewisinstitute.org/webfm_send/414

Humility, Andrew Murray

6b) Loving God & Neighbor

"Loving God with Heart and Mind," by Alistair McGrath. *Knowing & Doing*, C.S. Lewis Institute, Winter 2002. http://www.cslewisinstitute.org/webfm_send/615

"Following Jesus Christ," by Tom Tarrants. *Knowing & Doing*, C.S. Lewis Institute, Fall 2011. http://www.cslewisinstitute.org/webfm_send/846

"Argument from Agape," by Art Lindsley. *Knowing & Doing*, C.S. Lewis Institute, Winter 2007. http://www.cslewisinstitute.org/webfm_send/395

The Four Loves, C.S. Lewis

7) Authority of the Bible

"Is the Content of the Biblical Manuscripts Reliable?," by Amy Orr-Ewing. *Knowing & Doing*, C.S. Lewis Institute, Winter 2006. http://www.cslewisinstitute.org/webfm_send/621

"Christ and the Bible," by Art Lindsley. *Knowing & Doing*, C.S. Lewis Institute, Summer 2007. http://www.cslewisinstitute.org/webfm_send/423

Is the New Testament Reliable?, Paul Barnett

8) The Practice of Prayer

"Prayer: Worship & Adoration," by J. Oswald Sanders. *Knowing & Doing*, C.S. Lewis Institute, Spring 2004. http://www.cslewisinstitute.org/webfm_send/651

"Prayer: Thanksgiving," by J. Oswald Sanders. *Knowing & Doing*, C.S. Lewis Institute, Summer 2004. http://www.cslewisinstitute.org/webfm_send/652

Prayer Power Unlimited, J. Oswald Sanders

Christian Disciplines for the Christian Life, Donald Whitney

Letters to Malcolm, C.S. Lewis

9) The Mission of the Church

"In Christ; The Meaning and Implications of the Gospel of Christ," by John R.W. Stott. *Knowing & Doing*, C.S. Lewis Institute, Summer 2007.
http://www.cslewisinstitute.org/webfm_send/276

The Holy Spirit, Billy Graham

10) Sharing the Good News

"Evangelical, but not Evangelistic," by Stuart McAllister. *Knowing & Doing*, C.S. Lewis Institute, Spring 2009. http://www.cslewisinstitute.org/webfm_send/451

Why Jesus?, Nicky Gumbel

1. The LORD is compassionate and gracious, slow to anger, abounding in love. (Psalm 103:8, NIV)

2. For God so loved the world that he gave his one and only Son, that whoever believes in him shall not perish but have eternal life. For God did not send his Son into the world to condemn the world, but to save the world through him. (John 3:16–17, NIV)

3. For it is by grace you have been saved, through faith—and this is not from yourselves, it is the gift of God— not by works, so that no one can boast. (Ephesians 2:8–9, NIV)

4. To the church of God in Corinth, to those sanctified in Christ Jesus and called to be his holy people, together with all those everywhere who call on the name of our Lord Jesus Christ. (1 Corinthians 1:2, NIV)

5. Then he called the crowd to him along with his disciples and said: "If anyone would come after me, he must deny himself and take up his cross and follow me. For whoever wants to save his life will lose it, but whoever loses his life for me and for the gospel will save it." (Mark 8:34–35, NIV)

6a. Do nothing out of selfish ambition or conceit, but in humility consider others better than yourselves. Each of you should look not only to your own interests, but also to the interests of others. (Philippians 2:3–4, NIV)

6b. "Teacher, which is the greatest commandment in the Law?" Jesus replied: "'Love the Lord your God with all your heart and with all your soul and with all your mind.' This is the first and greatest commandment. And the second is like it: 'Love your neighbor as yourself.' All the Law and the Prophets hang on these two commandments." (Matthew 22:36–40, NIV)

7. All Scripture is God-breathed and is useful for teaching, rebuking, correcting and training in righteousness, so that the servant of God may be thoroughly equipped for every good work. (2 Timothy 3:16–17, NIV)

8. Be joyful always; pray continually, give thanks in all circumstances, for this is God's will for you in Christ Jesus. (1 Thessalonians 5:16–18, NIV)

9. Then Jesus came to them and said, "All authority in heaven and on earth has been given to me. Therefore go and make disciples of all nations, baptizing them in the name of the Father and of the Son and of the Holy Spirit, and teaching them to obey everything I have commanded you. And surely I am with you always, to the very end of the age." (Matthew 28:18–20, NIV)

10. But you will receive power when the Holy Spirit comes on you; and you will be my witnesses in Jerusalem, and in all Judea and Samaria, and to the ends of the earth. (Acts 1:8, NIV)

21704494R10102